∞

Relationships for Life

HOW CONSCIOUS LOVE
TRANSCENDS CRISIS, PAIN
AND SELF AVOIDANCE

FRANK NATALE

Edited by Ralph Cissne. Cover design by Wendy Saade.

Published by Morgan Road.

Library of Congress Control Number: 2014944787

ISBN-13: 978-0-9701443-4-8
ISBN-10: 0-9701443-4-2

"...in seeking these qualities, you will gain an opportunity for greater awareness of your self, which is the highest achievement any of us can accomplish at any given moment."

– Frank Natale

Contents

Forward

This book is based on Frank Natale's lifetime of experience helping tens of thousands of people transform their relationships and manifest greater clarity, creativity and achievement in their lives. The original version, *Mastering Alive Relationships*, was first published in 1990 and included vignettes from Frank's life along with select self-discovery exercises. Prior to his passing in 2002 Frank requested an abridged version be edited to focus on the 20 qualities presented here. "Let's get to the point," he said. And that's what has been done.

A gifted teacher, Frank studied and worked with many leaders of the modern human consciousness movement including Charles Dederich, Abraham Maslow, Carl Rodgers, Fritz Perls, Baba Muktananda, J. Krishnatmurti and Buckminster Fuller. In 1967 he was a cofounder of Phoenix House in New York, one of the world's largest residential treatment programs for chemical dependency. After twelve years as clinical director Frank chose to leave Phoenix House and concentrate his work on serving successful functioning personalities who wanted to improve the quality of their communications and relationships.

Frank began teaching experiential seminars, founded The Natale Institute and, over the following twenty years, developed a body of work he described as designed for "Individuals willing to see their problems as self-imposed limits, who choose to move beyond those limitations to create a higher level of consciousness and enjoyment in their lives." The 20 qualities presented in this book were the foundation of the Natale Relationships seminar series.

For those of us who studied with Frank, and presented his work, it was a privilege and an extraordinary opportunity to be of service to others. Frank challenged each of us to realize our aspirations, to be effective human beings and to make a difference. The lessons found in these 20 qualities of what Frank called "alive relationships" will empower you to let go of negative thought processes, discover a greater understanding of your self and, ultimately, make conscious choices about how you want to live your life. Enjoy.

With love and all it truly means,

Ralph Cissne

Introduction

After years of teaching relationships courses to thousands of students my intention with this book is to allow you to turn to any page and learn something new about relationships or at least discover something new about what you already know.

The qualities described in this book are found in personal or romantic situations, the two areas of life that receive the most attention, but they are also evident or lacking in our relationships with money, religion, sex, health, work and authority. In fact, they are the indicators of the status of your relationship with everything that is a part of your life. And it is the overall quality of your life that determines your self-esteem and personal power, integrity, ethics and your standards. In all of these areas you have more choices than you think. These qualities, of course, may be present in varying degrees in your life now and this book is not intended for you to judge or keep score. Some of these qualities may not be present at all and please do not suppose that they should be.

This book provides you with distinct guidelines for gaining access to keys that unlock doors. The more doors you pass through, the more positive will be the effect on your life and the more effective your life will be. Ultimately, in seeking these qualities, you will gain an opportunity for greater awareness of your self, which is the highest achievement any of us can accomplish at any given moment.

The purpose of this book is for you to take a look at you, to evaluate where you are in your relationships and where you are genuinely willing to be. It is designed to help you achieve or strengthen those vital signs that are part of what I prefer to call "alive" relationships. It provides the opportunity for you to learn how to create rather than to blame.

Creating or strengthening these "alive" characteristics demands making choices, being aware of your actions and thoughts, then transforming them. Take your time with this book, with your choices and with your transformation. And enjoy the results. Use these ideas for they are yours now. If you do, your old beliefs will crumble and your limitations will dissolve. Reach for the highest in yourself in all your relationships and empower others to do the same. Most importantly, enjoy and celebrate all of your relationships.

As love,

Frank Natale

∞

Creating "Alive" Relationships

We live in fast times. Our personal environment changes sometimes abruptly and significantly. Forms alter and shift. Appearances whirl in and out like mosaics in a kaleidoscope. Facades flash by like billboards. And in the process of this intense and constant change, technological, social, evolutionary, it seems that half of us are looking for a relationship and half of us are running away from one.

Little wonder that in this age of transformation, of everything as we know it, the obvious aspects of relationships are easily overlooked. Little wonder that a lot of our relationships turn out the way we have unconsciously envisioned them. It is also not surprising that a great many people in our society have, and co-exist within the confines of, relationships that are deader than a cold Big Mac.

Without our relationships we would not exist. The qualities of aliveness found in our relationships determine the quality of our existence. The intention of this book is to show you how to identify these qualities, which may or may not be present in your relationships. It also points the way to adding any or all of these qualities to your life. This book will affect the manner in which you view your relationships. It will help you assess these vital signs of relationship and make the choice to acquire them.

A truly alive relationship exists when we play with reality and allow it to play with us in the same way a tennis player hits the ball over the net and then, on the return, the ball creates when and how the player must respond. This play of creation and re-creation between the two players is what keeps the game alive and going strong. One player does not stand still hitting the ball back to the other player. On the return each player must move to the ball. They must change their point of view in order to stay alive and in the game. This is the same interactive play that must happen in order to create a relationship that is truly alive. The key is the harmonious play that occurs between you and whomever, or whatever, you choose. The result is the creation of aliveness essential to any healthy relationship.

The best business managers don't get paid to maintain the status quo. Their job is to develop new products, open new territory, increase company morale and profits. The dynamics of aliveness is vital to any thriving enterprise or relationship. I've witnessed many personal relationships flourish in the excitement of early stage aliveness. Then they settle down or marry and begin to define each other to death, framing the relationship in tiresome belief systems until they are perfect and trapped in expectations of themselves and others close to them. In this book you will find new choices that are now available to you. And the odds are good that you'll be a happier person within or without your present relationships.

The relationships that you have may be very alive, but may resemble the walking wounded or terminally ill. My suggestion is that you do not dwell on the dead parts. Dead relationships can and often do occur between children and their parents, lovers and their partners, employees and their employers. There are reasons for this, but they are not relevant here. What is relevant and necessary is to focus on the positive result. The path to aliveness in relationships is not to focus on the dead part. That's like going to the morgue to meet someone. Focus on the parts that are alive. The proper approach is not to spend all of your time examining what is wrong with you. The proper approach is to pay close attention to what is right with you. Focus, and then refocus, on those parts. This doesn't mean you should avoid what is unwanted. Simply choose to think in terms of "solution" rather than "dissolution."

Choose to take the bridge that will bring you farther across the river and closer to where you are willing to be. When you concentrate on what is wrong you are impotent, frigid and petrified. Strategically, for your own welfare, it is an error to focus on the dead part where pain has become a familiar psychological comfort zone. Dwelling on the pain and crisis is the avoidance of self. The familiar pain and crisis also attracts the most attention, which we frequently mistake for love and friendship. In contrast, to accelerate your aliveness is to make the choice to think and to focus your awareness on what you are willing to have in life. That is the bridge. That is the connection. That is the consciousness that guides you across and moves you forward. The way you create life is to look at what is right and ask, "How do I create more of that?" Then you make conscious choices to let go of what does not serve and embrace what does.

When you refuse to focus on your negative baggage whatever is unwanted begins to disappear. When you refuse to nurture, support or agree with the roots of negativity the roots will rot from lack of attention. Alive relationships are those relationships in which relating continues. To cut off that relating in an attempt to preserve a relationship is literally to kill it. Alive relationships are those in which the definition of "love" has been elevated to its proper place.

Love is the only constant, the only reality, and when you accept and understand that you will know it. One of the ways to get that love, of course, is through relationships. That's why we chase after someone with whom we think we are in love, someone who pushes the right buttons, who allows us to experience ourselves as love. Our problems begin when we start trying to define and mould our future happiness around that wonderful experience. We want to make sure it "stays around." Remember that love is love and an experience is something that is happening now. When you begin to experience saying, "I love you" as a statement about yourself rather than about the one you are addressing, your relationships will transform into a state of conscious love.

Few people actually focus on the quality of their relationships. Rather, they seem more concerned with their length. Anniversaries are big deals in relationships. We've all experienced or witnessed the judgments, even condemnations, put upon someone for leaving a relationship or ending that connection, even with a friend, much less a wife or husband.

Yet little thought is given in condemning them to celebrate their 17th anniversary with a hidden grimace. They remain trapped and bound by their own comforting devices in dead, nonproductive relationships, which in turn transfers a state of disease that impacts all of their other relationships. Consider there is no long-term reason for a relationship other than to love, serve, provide recreation and/or take care of one another. All other reasons or rationales will change. You can count on it because that's your experience.

When preserved and analyzed excessively, your relationship loses the quality of relating and becomes stagnant. You are now "a relationship." Verbs become nouns. Action slows down, and in some cases, totally ceases to exist. You may be able to identify some of your own relationships that have been pressed into a non-relating mold. If you also find yourself petrified about a particular relationship this may mean that you are terrified and resentful of that person, the same one whom you believe you love, respect or enjoy. You are stuck in a conclusion and can't escape. An "alive" relationship is a direction that cannot be mistaken for a conclusion.

One of the keys to an alive relationship is to refocus the relationship on a regular basis. To do this you need to stay in present time. You need to be aware, alert and open to experience. When you define or allow yourself to be defined know that you have concluded that you and your relationship are blocked from aliveness. As far as that relationship is concerned, you're dead. Remember that you cannot define anything until it is framed in time and therefore stopped. And yet everything is constantly transforming and changing and you cannot communicate an accurate definition of that. A running horse is a changing horse. Each time you try to communicate what it is, it is not anymore. Each time you get into a relationship and define it, it is not anymore. You smugly embrace your assumption, massage your definition, and scratch your head trying to figure out why it does not work. "What went wrong?" you ask. What usually goes wrong is that you did not consider that relationships continue to exist and continue to transform much the same as your body. You can try to corral them and keep them all tidy inside your well-constructed definition, but what you are really doing is defining each other into a state of complete boredom, fear and walking death.

You can play that game. A lot of people do. If you don't think so, think of the endless flow of "How to Save Your Marriage" magazine articles you've seen. You don't have to play that game and, therefore, you can have a lot more fun with your relationships. For starters you can simply recognize that all of your relationships are now transforming and enjoy the show. This book shows you how to do that.

It is helpful if you think of this as a non-description. In each of the following I describe one of the vital signs of an alive relationship. These are indicative qualities of an alive relationship and not an alive relationship itself. They may or may not be present. All of them, however, seem to be variously evident in those relationships I have most admired:

Alive: You having life, you having spirit, you living, you in existence, you alert, you aware, you intelligent, you transforming, you changing.

An alive relationship: Love without attachment, an environment in which individuals flourish, an awareness of another person's way of being, a related way of being.

A related way of being: Related, but not possessed. It is easy to get the impression in loving relationships, and in any other relationship, that if you are the boss you possess your wife, your employees and your children. What is actually going on is that – if you are in one of those roles – your wife, your employees and your children are serving you. In reality you own no relationship. It is important to notice the distinction between a related way of being and a possessed or controlled way of being. And it should be easy to notice because most people are owned by their relationships. Their money owns them. They are owned by their careers. Their husbands or wives control them. Their parents control them. Their children possess them.

Most people are not in a related way of being. They do not realize that they are separate. In fact, they unconsciously behave and think as if they are chained inextricably together. If a parent-child relationship never grows beyond the parent-child stage – if it remains the same over the years – it dies, caught in the melodrama of control, possession and too often desperate clinging. Unfortunately, this is the case with the majority of such relationships and the pain doesn't go away.

On the other hand, when parents and children continue to relate, a state of aliveness continues to be present within their relationship. This allows them to transform from a parent-child relationship to one of having a mother and father who are intimate old friends. These are the kind of friends who can chronicle your life with detail and compassion unlike any other friend. When you begin to experience relationships at that level you will begin to have extraordinary, wonderful and joyous relationships.

Alive relationships are about a related way of being, not a controlled way of being or a possessed way of being. Instead of being forced into a time-and-space definition they are free and open to experience. Notice the distinction, and by keeping it in mind, it will begin to become habit. Your relationships will begin to become what you create instead of what you have been accepting.

An awareness of another person's way of being: Awareness is unfocused thought and not to be confused with the judgment of another's actions. It is not a focused definition, but rather an allowance of how that person is. Awareness is intelligence not yet actualized, recognition not necessarily shaped into words. A child has a better understanding of awareness than most adults. A child's spontaneous creativity is reflected in their imaginary playmates and their ability to step beyond definition to see the world as they wish. But they slowly and gradually lose their awareness, magic and creativity. They lose them because these qualities, which are inborn traits, receive insufficient nurturing. As they grow up and begin to learn the ways of adults, they are taught to focus their thought on what is necessary to assure their survival.

This generally comes through in the form of parenting, the survival training job that we have yet to do consciously and effectively without damaging our children's creativity, self-esteem and aliveness. Little wonder that generation after generation of children grow up with less self-esteem than they deserve, leading uncreative lives and getting stuck in dull, boring and unstable relationships. To be in an alive relationship requires being conscious and alert. It demands the courage to change and to accept change in all things, including those you love. Because you have been trained to do otherwise, you have to keep reminding yourself. After a while, by paying attention, it becomes habitual. You begin to stop unconsciously defining people. You begin to realize that the person you are looking at is not you, but rather a whole new adventure. And you are very grateful that you are able to hold their hand every once in a while or that they will share themselves with you. Ultimately, with practice at a new awareness, you discover that you may know very little about them, which is why they are so exciting.

An awareness of another person's way of being: This is to accept that what you know about this person is minimal. You also begin to realize that you are in a relationship to discover each other, not to define each other. And when you comprehend this you start having extraordinary relationships. They are adventurous and childlike. In fact, you may first experience it more with children because they are more alive. They naturally make the choice to live. They have not unconsciously chosen the death process yet. They have not figured out the shortest way to drive to work and they have not been driving that route for twenty years. They get lost once in a while, walk down a different street and experience discovery. They think differently. They are aware. They are available. They are open. To have relationships that are alive you must reclaim that. You must make the choice to think and to be alive. When you reclaim your aliveness you will begin to allow the people in your relationships to reclaim theirs. When that happens, you will not need to know what is going to happen all the time. It is a little frightening at first and then it comes to be a lot of fun. The fear also transforms into something you'll really like. It's called excitement.

An environment in which individuals flourish: We are talking about an environment not a focused or defined space. Environments are expandable. They are changeable. Environments surround you and you become a part of them. You become one with them. Your experience is being in them. Another characteristic of environments is that no matter how many times you go into them they are never the same. Just take the time to experience. Every sunrise and every sunset is different every day of your life. The grass is a little longer. You hear, smell and feel different things. Your unique emotional state has much to do with how you perceive and react to your environment. In fact, you are a participator not an observer. You are in a relationship with your environment, the kind of relationship that depends on your awareness of what's going on around you.

To achieve an alive relationship you must have an environment in which individuals can flourish. It is important for you to recognize that individuals cannot flourish in a defined space. Only in an environment can an individual truly be a lover, a friend, a business consultant, a partner, a competitor, a teacher, a student and still be an individual. Notice the word "individual." It takes two or more participants in a relationship to relate. The choice of an individual to attend a particular school, to worship a particular religion, to live in a particular geographic location or to experience a certain lifestyle tends to draw an unconscious stereotype. With unconscious judgments the person is now a preppy, a hillbilly, a yuppie, etc. We obsessively cast a group label on every individual we encounter. Although we seem to be naturally obsessed by such categorizations, the individuals with whom we relate are always unique within their chosen contexts.

When you experience people as individuals your whole experience of relationships changes dramatically. You understand that most people think once they've joined with other people they become a group. You begin to be careful not to continually think of yourself as a spouse, a parent, a friend, an employer, an employee or whatever it is. These are labels on a can. They are unconscious definitions that limit creativity and pleasure. Remember, regardless of how many people you know, that you are still you. When you consciously choose to be yourself in a relationship you will be alive. You will experience individuality. You will have people being who they are and there will be an exchange of thoughts, emotions and growth. Such an environment allows you to just be you, an individual with many identities and many relationships. And it allows you to see others the same way. It's a refreshing and satisfying way to look at what's going on around you.

An environment in which individuals flourish: Flourish means to grow vigorously. When you are in a relationship in which you are not growing vigorously, it is vital that you reexamine your reasons for being in that relationship. If you are in school and you are not learning, what are you doing? If you are in a romantic and sexual relationship and you are not experiencing romance and sexual satisfaction, what are you doing? If you are in a relationship because of fun and recreation and you not having a good time, what are you doing? If you experience your career as just a job rather than as meaningful service, what are you doing? If you are a member of an organized religion and you are not growing spiritually, what's the point? What is the purpose of each of your relationships? For what purpose are you in them? Parental approval? Group acceptance? Or are you in them for the spiritual sanction of your preacher or guru, priest or rabbi?

If you are not growing in your relationships, they are not fully alive. Growth, in fact, is the purpose of relationships. And to grow vigorously is the key to creating alive relationships. This means that you may grow out of a relationship as well as grow within one. Mark Twain left school, he said, when it began to interfere with his education. What Mark Twain sought, and what I am talking about, is flourishing aliveness. It does not mean that you run away from every relationship you have that is absent of growth because you have obviously contributed to the lack of aliveness present. It is not about blaming. It is about dealing with your own inability to flourish and your own lack of aliveness. It's about you being honest with yourself and being courageous enough to do something about it. It means that you honestly look and ask yourself important questions:

"What contribution am I *not* making to my career?"

"What contribution am I *not* making to my marriage?"
"What contribution am I *not* making to my education?"
"How am I withholding?"

With this new level of clarity and intent, you can either choose to contribute and grow in that relationship or you can leave it with dignity.

Relationship is love without attachment: That may sound simple, but it is not easy to do. It is definitely not the way most people enter and try to maintain a loving relationship, which is one reason why so many marriages fail or stagnate. If you are experiencing difficulties within your relationships the initial barrier may be that you, like most people, do not experience yourself as love. You have created relationships that are tangible or "real" while dragging along the negative thoughts you associate with those realities.

Your relationships are a mirror reflection of you and a means to experience your self in a tangible way. If you think something is wrong with your relationships, it is time to stop pointing your finger at your wife, husband, child or boss. It is time to look inside and say, "They are reflections of me. What am I doing?" Or, "What have I been doing for years that causes them to be that way?" This is an opportunity to see who you are and to grow. It is a chance to experience yourself as love, which is what you are at the intangible level when you are absent of negative thought.

Love, given definition and unconsciously attached to anything or anyone, ceases to be love. Love is sufficient unto itself. It cannot be attached to anything. It is intangible. It is a state of consciousness. Your need to make it tangible makes this miraculous movement waver and become inhibited. Start being conscious when you attach love to something or someone and notice the conditions you place on that attached love. When you were born your mother and father loved you unconditionally. At some point they realized they had this significant responsibility, or job, called parenting. And as you became aware of this parenting role, from your point of view, love became conditional. It became:

"I love you if you make good grades."
"I love you if you do your chores."
"I love you if you get to bed on time."

This is what you perceived whether it was communicated verbally or not. It was at that point that you began to feel that the only love you knew or wanted was being pulled out from under you. Before that, they just loved you unconditionally. You were sufficient unto yourself. You were enough as yourself. Their love was not attached to anything because it was sufficient unto itself. To this day most people go on repeating this destructive pattern with their children, husbands, wives and lovers. What mothers and fathers must begin to say is: "We love you. We always will love you. We have this job, which is essential to your survival and we need your cooperation. It is called parenting. It is our job to teach you to focus and function effectively with the least amount of damage to you and we want you to participate in this responsibility. And together, we will do the best we can."

This is conscious communication. This is conscious love. It does not attach love to parenting. Love is love. Parenting is parenting. Your children will hear that and, although they may not understand at first, they will in time be grateful for having been given the opportunity to contribute to their own identity. Unfortunately, that is not the norm. Parents traditionally communicate unconscious and familiar refrains such as: "Grow up. Stop acting like a child. You don't appreciate me. Where did I go wrong? Stop crying or I'll give you something to cry about."

We need to move away from this unconscious way of communication because it creates a ticking time bomb that is highly destructive to any relationship, beyond that of the parent and child. Be clear that love attached to anything ceases to be conscious love and becomes unconscious love and unconscious manipulation, which eventually becomes aggressive or submissive exploitation. By knowing the difference between conscious love and unconscious love in your relationships you will begin to create a new aliveness in them and in you.

By examining the vital signs of alive relationships in the following chapters, keep in mind that: An alive relationship is love without attachment, an environment that empowers individuals to flourish, an awareness of another person's way of being, a related way of being.

∞

Quality 1

Being Responsible to Each Other

Most of us learn to be responsible "for" people not "to" them and though we are well intentioned this kind of responsibility inevitably leads to resentment. Children eventually respond by blaming their parents for limiting them or for not allowing them to demonstrate their capabilities.

Although I've refined this principle as part of my work, I first learned about keeping agreements from my mother. She had certain agreements, as mother's have, and when she made those clear to me I kept them. On a deeper level, I learned that keeping agreements was a way to be responsible to the people who cared for me. This was also a way to show my mother that I loved her without surrendering my freedom and dignity. When people keep their agreements they don't experience a lot of drama. They have time to focus on their aliveness and adventure.

Responsible: The willingness to respond to each other rather than to be accountable. Present time. Now.

Being responsible to someone is another way of being accurate.

And:

- Accuracy is a form of love.
- Accuracy is a function of caring.

When you care about others:

- You are accurate with them.
- You are precise.
- You don't gossip or distort information.
- You don't embellish.
- You are straight.

Mature, conscious love creates the permission to be your self. When you love others on that level you are honest with them. What you are more likely to see in our society is dependent, unconscious love, which demands dishonesty and self-denial. However well intentioned we believe ourselves to be, we generally experience difficulty keeping our agreements. This breakdown occurs because we usually have been required to agree unconsciously to too many people, therefore:

- Lighten up your agreements.
- Create agreement only on those issues that are essential to the survival of your relationships.
- And, in any one relationship, never exceed three survival agreements.

When we are responsible to each other in our relationships we create freedom, support and fun. These are the benefits that come naturally from the experience of keeping one's agreements.

Unfortunately, most of us are caught in a more common and inequitable arrangement. Rather than agree to an alive and growing relationship, which is absent of form, we try to press it into a form that we think it should be. We attempt to secure these inherited models for relationship, in time attaching ourselves to them with all the fervor and intention of a leech. Rather than allowing freedom, we attempt to control each other. Then we are compelled to initiate some form of constant accountability and end up being forced to be responsible for each other. Our agreements then crumble into rationales for breaking them, creating stagnation and guilt, anger and no fun at all.

Responsible: The ability to go for the highest in all your relationships, while knowing where you are, rather than relating though unconscious tunnel vision and anxiety. Clarity about where you are willing to go in your relationships, while you appreciate where you are presently, is the secret to creating alive relationships. Most of us, when we really take a close look at our relationships will eventually conclude that we have not learned the skills to create that clarity. We therefore do not create agreement. Without clarity agreement is impossible.

Instead, we tend to destroy our relationships and the opportunity to let aliveness blossom naturally. We eventually become intolerant of what we have. Confronted with the smallest disagreement or disappointment, we are screaming and yelling and threatening to leave. When our agreements are simple and clear there is a level of freedom and of trust, which nurtures relationship. It is this same level of simplicity and clarity at which we create humor and lightness.

To be responsible to each other is vital. It takes a while to learn "how to be responsible to" because you have been taught by example to be in control of another person or to be accountable to another person. This lesson is important and requires constant awareness. In a relationship that is alive you keep your agreements. If you find you cannot, then that agreement needs to be redefined or dropped entirely. Reviewing your agreements regularly, and updating them, is essential to creating and nurturing alive relationships.

∞

Quality 2

Responsiveness and Existential Living

All of my teachers were honest and present in the moment. Karl Pribram, a man of great scientific achievement, was more playful in his seventies than most children. Baba Muktananda, an incredibly powerful spiritual master, was one of the most innocent and playful teachers I have known. His childlike energy always communicated knowingness. There are many others in my life that exemplified the qualities of existential living and I loved them all. That is what responsiveness is about: being in love with it all in the moment.

Responsiveness: The ability to respond, rather than to react, in present time.

Existential living: To set your direction rather than be singularly goal oriented. Existential living is to be absent of pretence and, therefore, to be absent of form. Existential living is an experiential quality.

It requires you to:

- Be open to experience and change.
- Relate in the moment.
- Operate as little as possible from memory.
- Live in present time.
- Allow your relationships to transform with or without you.

When you are in an alive relationship, you become more and more aware that life is existential. This relationship is a moment-by-moment experience that is in a continuous state of change. When you are in an alive relationship:

- You do not expect everyone to remain with you.
- You will let people go and experience others.
- You know that people always come into your life to make their contribution.
- You actively make contributions to each other, which are whole and complete at any given moment.

You cannot move beyond present time. You can only be in it. At this level of experience present time is the future. The fear you feel is your aliveness. Make fear your friend, embrace your fear and rename it excitement. Face the fact that life is a risk. It is existential. When it gets dangerous, you can always go back to the past, to the comfort zone and to the familiar. Your life experience will always be there. But to live in the past is to meet death before you die, and to destroy everyone and everything with whom you relate.

- To relate in the past is to be committed to death.
- To relate in the present is to be committed to living.

It is your choice. The secret to this process is to stay "in the fear" until it transforms into excitement, then step out and scare yourself again. Many of us do not want to do this. We want to stay in the comfort zone even though the comfort zone that we accept is all too familiar and painful.
- Existential living frightens because it has the potential for danger.
- Experience the discomfort and after a while it is no longer fear.
- It is excitement.

You must keep reminding yourself to stay in present time, because nearly everyone around you dwells in the past. Of course, nostalgia can be fun. It is okay to retreat into the past as long as you have retreated by choice, as long as you don't confuse that occasional choice for life and as long as it's not an avoidance of being in the now. The past is a respite. It is a "time out" and an opportunity to realize that life is never over, it only transforms to new levels.

The ability to "respond rather than to react" requires considerable awareness and practice before it is internalized. This is a conscious skill. I practiced this skill for years and finally just let go. Letting go allowed me to realize being responsive involves being in the moment. It involves forgetting in present time. Responsiveness involves:

- You operating more from present time and less from memory.
- Not worrying.
- You don't forget your skills or your experience.
- You only drop the conditions that surround them.
- Responsiveness is accepting that you are never upset for the reason you think. You cannot be upset in present time because when you are in present time, you are alert to the irrefutable fact that life is a new experience, a wonder to behold.
- Emotional upsets are always a reaction to something left incomplete with something or someone in the past.

You being upset in the moment may be directed toward the person who has been aggravating you for years and at whom you finally scream. But it is you who have been withholding that upset and therefore approving that person's behavior. When you become aware of yourself reacting, stop. Be aware and focus on what is going on. It is never what it appears to be. It may be from a week ago, or twenty-five years ago, but it is not simply because of what is happening now. In fact, there is no upset in present time, only pleasure and aliveness.

There has long been recognition in both psychology and religion that truth is the only way to experience present time, but truth aligns you immediately with your environment. Most religions and therapies don't tell you that. They prefer you to figure it out for yourself on the premise that you may not be intelligent enough to value or to use the information. This approach, in which you may subject yourself to years of discipleship, does not advance your quest for alive relationships.

Truth will always put you in present time and will eliminate any upsets in that moment. All you have to do is to learn how to tell the truth, which is not as easy as it sounds. There are two secrets to truth:

- The saying "To always tell the truth is to your advantage." is not true. The truth is, it is always to your advantage to tell your self the truth.
- The skill of truth is to tell your self the truth faster. Faster than whomever or whatever you are relating to; then you are responding, not reacting.
- When you respond, you have the advantage in life.
- Responsiveness is the key to mastery of your life.

When you respond you don't experience other people's reactions to you as your responsibility. Equally important, when someone responds to you, you know it and you appreciate that person.
- The challenge in learning how to respond is that the brain does not think in present time.
- The brain is absent of thought in present time.
- Thoughts are always about the past and the future.

Thinking in terms of the past and the future is how we have been trained to use our minds so that we can master our environment. As time passes, we forget how to be absent of thought, as we often were as children. Children live more in present time than we do. They move from one experience to another, from one moment to another. For this reason children are more accepting of their immediate environment.

You have been conditioned to operate from your future and your past, neither of which has anything to do with your reality right now. In fact the future is based on the past. This means that you re-create the past in new forms, which is why most of us grow old and bored with life. If you continue to think this way eventually your relationships grind to a screeching halt and become totally absent of all creativity and aliveness. Being out of present time is unconscious and counter productive. Present time is synonymous with aliveness. It's your choice.

∞

Quality 3

Thought Is Creative

Engage your mind. It is the ultimate source of your creativity and aliveness. Your mind empowers you to construct yourself and others with your thoughts. When you are aware and accept this you understand:

- Your reality and your relationships do not exist independent of you.
- You are a participator and therefore the creator of your relationships.

The way in which you look at something determines what it is to you. The way in which you look at something creates your experience. The physical world is constantly changing depending on how you view it.

Your perception of things is what creates them. Consider:

- Be willing to live your life fully and you will die satisfied.
- Anyone who is afraid to die is afraid to live.
- Focus on how you are willing to have your relationships.
- And you will create it.
- If you think: "life is a struggle" you will die proving it.

The brain and the mind are different. Your thoughts do not originate in your brain. The thoughts you call up are the ones you have already received, which are stored in your brain's memory. The goal is to create new thoughts and let go of those thoughts that are worn out and useless. To think that thoughts originate in your brain is as naive as thinking that there are people and places in your television set. The more powerful your antennae the more stations you receive. Expand to a satellite dish and you can access television worldwide. But if all you have are "rabbit ears" on your head you only receive local stations and believe that is all that is available.

The brain is a physical organ, located between your ears, and will die with the body. Your mind is meta-physical and defies definition. Your mind is everywhere and in everything and will live on long after your body expires, but the brain is like a radio station capable of receiving and transmitting data it pulls from the thousands of signals. The more conscious we are the more related and alive we become.

- Open your mind.
- Clear your brain on a regular basis.
- Let go of old beliefs and points of view, which do not support you.

Abandon points of view that take up space and keep new thoughts from entering your consciousness. When you do this you will create thoughts that manifest an aliveness you have not experienced since childhood. Empty your brain. You just have to let go and be available to new thoughts, which will create you and your relationships in present time.

Your emotions are created by the way you think about them. When you engage the mind you consciously perceive those emotions and are able to transform fear into excitement. Fear is simply inexperienced excitement. As soon as you master a particular fear it becomes excitement then you are free to go out and scare yourself again by doing something more frightening. In relationships we often hear people say, "I've been hurt twice and that's it. I quit." Where is the consciousness in that?

The way in which you define an emotion determines what that emotion will be. It is all about how you perceive the feeling. When you are conscious boredom becomes serenity. Your point of view chooses what to call it. Boredom is thinking there is nothing worth doing. Serenity is experienced in knowing everything is worth doing, but in the moment you choose to just be present. Boredom and serenity are the same emotion. It just depends on how you choose to think about them.

As fear can transform to excitement, as boredom can move toward serenity, loneliness can become solitude. Loneliness is how some perceive being alone and many people are terrified of being alone. But if you really consider loneliness carefully it transforms into being alone or "all one" and it becomes solitude. Loneliness is not the absence of something or someone. Loneliness is the absence of self. We have all experienced feeling lonely while in a room full of people or lying in bed next to our lover.

We are thought itself. Our brains construct what we call our relationships. Our relationships do not exist independent of our thoughts. To know and to have the direct experience of creating all your relationships is to experience integrity in all of your relationships. When you take responsibility for your thoughts integrity occurs and eliminates circumstance. Your parents or children suddenly cease to be circumstances with which you are stuck. Thoughts such as "We had to get married" and "We stayed together for the children" become outmoded ways of thinking. Victim-hood falls away. You are no longer ill fated or fortunate, rather you experience the joy and the power that comes from creating your relationships.

Creative thinking enables:

- You to have clarity of purpose.
- You to be clear about the purpose of your relationships at any given time and therefore are able to cause them knowingly.
- Creates compassion as a form of love expression, an overt acknowledgment of your relationships and their contribution to your life.
- Creates affinity, which is the liking and loving for your relationships, the occupation of the same idea and experience.

Be creative. Be clear.

∞

Quality 4

The Choice to Think

The choice to think determines your reality. When you are conscious you have all the relationships you choose to have. When you choose to be healthy and prosperous you are clear about what your body requires and the direction your career is headed. With practice you learn to think faster and make clear choices, knowing you can always change your mind.

The choice to think: An alternative beyond decision, the experience of moving into the unknown with excitement rather than fear.

- To cause.
- To create.
- To survive.
- To prosper.

During the course of our lives our thoughts determine our relationships. As children we think creatively. In a gradual process by adulthood we go from creative thinking to defensive thinking. We stop making choices and make only one choice: the choice to survive. The choice to survive usually occurs at an early age when we are criticized for not effectively handling our environment. We begin to have thoughts about "not being good enough" or "being wrong." The list of such thoughts is long and you can add many of your own to this list. After a series of these thoughts we stumble into the choice not to think. Instead of finding life through conscious thought we create behavior patterns to avoid life.

We can reclaim our power and we can choose to think. Those who make this choice see more clearly than others who spend their entire lives avoiding loss and discomfort. The choice to think is the choice to live. It is what makes our species unique. The decision to avoid thinking is a commitment to disorder, death and disease. To avoid is to decide to be an extra in someone else's life and to think someone else's thoughts. When you have made the choice to think as an individual you express the following characteristics:

- You have clarity about your past, present and future. You prefer clarity rather than vague impressions about yourself.
- You value freedom and experience this as responsibility. You never use freedom as license.
- You take full responsibility for creating and receiving all of the results in your life. You don't play victim, blame or look for someone or something else to create your life for you.
- You go for the highest in yourself, playing the game of life at 100 percent. Rather than playing it safe and pretending to live your life in the comfort zone, you are willing to risk.
- You constantly move into present time, completing and forgiving. You do this rather than dragging on dead or dying relationships, feeling incomplete, playing avoidance games, being resentful or getting stuck in the past.
- You have long-term relationships. You choose to trust and accept that the transformation in your relationships is continuous, valuable and natural. You have flourishing alive relationships rather than an abundance of short relationships that dissolve when the slightest discomfort occurs, destroying those relationships before they transform.
- Change excites you. You experience transformation as the ability to have conscious experience beyond form. This is the opposite of being fearful of change.

Resisting change, and being defensive, causes you to experience transformation as "the end."

- You are accurate and courageous. You maintain your ethics and honor even under the threat of knowing that your truth is the doorway to your future. You choose to do that rather than to be "nice" and fearfully dishonest. You do that rather than turn your power over to others and become lost in random opinions, beliefs and feelings or suffer from chronic low self-esteem and helplessness.
- You have a commitment to excellence, going for mastery of everything you choose to do. You value your skills and acknowledge the skills of others. You are a counterpoint to those who are absent of real skill, training, experience or understanding and those who judge and "make wrong" others who view the acquisition of skill with passion and excitement.
- You trust your own body, mind, spirit and environment. You know that doubt, when experienced thoroughly, always transforms to self-trust. You recognize that those who have chosen not to think fear themselves, others and the "greater forces" they believe control them. You know that is how they allow themselves to become impotent and subject to "blind faith" rather than self-trust.

Life constantly confronts us with alternatives. The choices we make determine our sense of ourselves. We are the only species capable of rejecting and betraying our own minds, intelligence and aliveness. The extent to which we exercise our mind, or negate it directly, affects our relationship with ourselves, our family and our communities and ultimately the aliveness of our species and this planet.

Choice is creation. It is life itself and in life we are free to be anyone once we are aware of the choices. When we choose to sculpt ourselves the whole stone is available to us. We can sculpt a hero or a villain, a conscious creator or an unconscious victim. Our job is to choose to remove the unwanted chunks of stone while listening to our conscious self inside, screaming to be transformed and made visible to the world. If we don't accept that job then we go on living like weeds and driftwood as unconscious victims at the dubious mercy of our environment.

- You must remove the chunks of stone.
- You must move beyond fate and destiny.

As a sculptor works with their hands you must choose to use your mind to create your conscious self. You are creation, not an unconscious object at the mercy of known and unknown forces. Each of us is a capable and creative being who has been given the opportunity to become a miserable marriage partner or a wonderful lover, a serious lover or a joyous companion, a common rock or a great work of art. These choices are available to each of us.

Our brains constantly receive an incomprehensible number of thoughts. These thoughts are already there, meaning that they exist now, simultaneously, outside of our brain. We then filter and distinguish those we choose to create and cause knowingly. When we think at the level of choice we move beyond current understanding. We move to an alternative beyond decision. The choice to create our relationships is a willingness to go beyond solely what we want for ourselves. It is a commitment beyond our own limitations and barriers.

Inherent in the choice to think is commitment without effort and struggle. We get little external support for fun, playful, satisfying relationships that seem to be going nowhere. Instead we are encouraged to have significant, serious, meaningful, obligated relationships that are "going somewhere." Our choice to relate the way we do is constantly being challenged yet that choice is aliveness itself. That's been my experience and it works well for all my relationships. With the choice to think comes:

- Certainty, clarity of mind and direction.
- To know rather than to think.

My son knows I'm his father. He doesn't think about it. There is no questioning, no considering, no evaluating. We are certain about being father and son and therefore we are certain about having father and son situations, problems and goals that we have and enjoy within the context of our relationship. We are certain. Belief is unnecessary. The word "lief" means desire, so "belief" means the desire to be.

- When you know through your own experience you transcend belief.
- When you transcend belief to knowing in your relationships 90 percent of your problems disappear and those remaining can be solved without effort and struggle. Belief is required only when insufficient experience has occurred, when there is no certainty.
- Do you know or do you believe in God? Marriage? Love? Astrology? Vitamin supplements?

When you have made the choice to think:

- You transcend belief.
- You move beyond form.
- You move beyond organized religion, beyond gurus, beyond priests, beyond rabbis, beyond ministers. You move beyond the middlemen, beyond retail. You get whatever you choose wholesale.

You go directly to the God you know as you know yourself. The need for belief disappears. At that point, the person who tells you that there is no God has no impact. No person's logic, compounded rationale or implied scientific data will cause you uncertainty. The same is true of love, friendship and joy. You are beyond current understanding, beyond decision, beyond belief, beyond institution, biology and form. No one can convince you that your direct experience does not exist. Many of us do not choose to distinguish the difference between direct experience and memory of experience. We should. It is, for example, the difference between loving someone and telling them so, and operating from the memory of once having loved them.

The choice to think is:

- Metaphysical, formless, easy, unlimited and boundless.
- Recognition that thoughts are metaphysical things with the power to create or destroy matter.
- The commitment to be willing to transform into whatever form is necessary to relate and be in alive relationships.
- The willingness to be anything.

At this level of thought and creation all relationships are possible, perfect and available to you. At the level of choice it really only requires you to allow into your reality what is already there. All of the relationships already exist, therefore, any relationships that you choose you will have. That is why you have the relationships you have now. You chose them and you continue to choose them.

Whether your thought is conscious or unconscious you are still making the choice. Just because you are unconscious about creating your relationships does not mean you are not the person choosing to create them. You are just choosing them unconsciously and, as a result, you will probably continue to create more undesirable and unsatisfactory relationships.

The tendency is to hold onto your beliefs and your decisions with the result that you are "willing to be realistic." The problem with this is that anything defined as "realistic" has already happened, so it's really in the past. When you say, "Let's be realistic" or "Let's be reasonable," you are asking for agreement based on your beliefs, your decisions, your realism, your viewpoint and your past experiences. That kind of expectation leaves little room for openness to change and dissipates present time awareness. Being in a reasonable relationship is synonymous with being in a dead relationship. It's not only limited, it's boring. If you are coming from belief, or from being reasonable, you are coming from the latest lie.

Reasonable people are liars. They are dishonest. Reasonable relationships are also lies. Because of their dishonesty they will eventually crumble and fall away with enough blame left behind to satisfy the beliefs and reasonableness of the participants. Relationships at the level of belief and decision just change. Marriage and divorce happen repeatedly as the people change with the new form.

Relationships at the level of choice are creative. What you get here are lovers, friends and companions. The people involved create the new form and they transform.

Observe the consciousness of children, which you once had. They tire of playing a certain game, but choose to play a new game with the same playmates. They value the playmates more than the game. Adults tire of playing a certain game, such as marriage or lover, and choose to be separated, divorced, left or dumped. We egotistically value "winning the game" more than the person with whom we have been playing.

The choice to think is to:
- Create.
- Know.
- Generate.
- Innovate.
- Invent.
- Communicate.
- Notice something unseen about which we already know.

Listen closely and just visualize. See all of your relationships as being creative environments and spaces for you to notice something new, something previously not seen but that you understand and know. Then the games and the forms change and the people in alive relationships remain and transformation occurs.

Being in a relationship absent of choice is like driving when you don't know how, having one accident after another and blaming it on the car or other drivers. As goes the driving so goes the relationship. You start giving long, tedious explanations for your accidents such as:

- "Marriage doesn't really work."
- "I'm unable to be really intimate."
- "It's tough being a teenager."
- "It's tougher being a parent."
- "I'm a victim of divorce."
- "I'm a used and abused sexual partner."

The list goes on and often in elaborate and equally boring detail. Without the choice to think you have no choice but to be a victim. Unless you choose to change to choice you will always be living someone else's life. You will always be an extra in someone else's play. The choice to think allows you to make the distinction between:

- Direct experience and memory of experience.
- Knowing and knowledge.
- A master teacher and a book.
- Conscious intended communication and wanting to communicate.
- Being with the people who created you and "visiting" your parents.

A married man when asked, "Do you love your wife?" will usually respond, "Yes, I love my wife." But what he usually means is, "I live my life consistent with the memory of loving my wife," or even less redeeming, "I live my life consistent with the random past experiences of having enjoyed my wife." Notice how reasonable it gets and how dead it is. Unfortunately, this kind of deal ends up being, "I live my life consistent with the concept of 'I love you,' the direct experience of that is rare and I don't choose to make the distinction between the two." Your entire life becomes affected by the memory of experience, which engenders:

- Guilt.
- The struggle of being in a relationship.
- Feeling stuck and inadequate.
- Being critical and judgmental.

Therefore, your relationships consequently lack:

- Integrity.
- Sincerity.
- Compassion.
- Validation.
- Joy.
- Aliveness.

The next question you probably ask is, "How do I get into direct experience more?" The answer may not be easy, but it is simple. You make the choice to create your relationships until you're capable of conscious, continuous choice. You will find that this is not always a very popular way of operating because the victims of our society have a name for the flip side of choice. They call it rejection. The choice is simple. Either choose to have someone in your life who is always there waiting for you or take the risk and choose someone alive who won't be available to you all of the time because they are busy enjoying life.

It is as easy to get lost in the memory of experience, as it is to read a new menu and recall with delight when you enjoyed that food before. You order the dish believing it will taste as well, only to be disappointed with the poor quality. What is true, unfortunately, is that most of humanity views life as a very limited menu from which it is usually too expensive to order. This means that most read the menu a lot, but seldom experience eating the food. That is true except for those of us who trust that life is a banquet. It may not always be fair, but it is always abundant. People in New York believe they are eating Mexican food while people in Texas know they are. People in Texas believe they are eating Italian food while people in New York know they are. Life is about making the choice to know the difference between the menu and the food and then to stop eating the menu.

By the time most of us reach age forty our memory of experience dominates our lives until almost all of our direct experience is buried under the memory of experience. Few of the people you meet have new and fresh outlooks. Everything is the same or similar. Creating disappears. Unless you make a conscious choice to think and to know and experience growth you soon join the ranks of the upright walking dead. Whenever I recognize that this has happened to me I usually take a leap. I find a new career or a new home. I reinvent myself. The last time was the move from New York to live more in Europe.

Most of my friends frowned with disbelief saying, "You'll be back in three months." I returned fifteen years later to Hawaii smiling with the actual joy of the experience. Simply, the food of life is available if you choose to enjoy. Alive relationships and your ability to create them are always at hand.

Quality 5

Service and Acknowledgment

My experience of service began, as it does for most of us, with my mother. She was a classic Italian mother who took care of me and my father took care of us. As a child I was never concerned about anything. And throughout my life I have loved being cared for, provided the caring is absent of maternal control.

When anyone has been of service to me I have never forgotten. Service transcends time. And I have loved, acknowledged and stayed in touch with those who have been there for me. It's important that we are clear how service and acknowledgment contribute to consciousness.

Service: Synonymous with support – giving assistance or support to another while absent of judgment. True service is an act that transcends time and is done without expecting acknowledgement.

Acknowledgement: The awareness and ability to share publicly what and whom you value – to notice the people who contribute to your life.

Many reasons exist for a relationship. Whatever the reasons for the relationships in your life, you have created both the relationships and the reasons. It is important to:

- Be aware that the reasons will change.
- Know that being unaware of this may cause you to be upset.

People do change, especially people who are intelligent and alive. In the long term, every reason for your relationships changes except one. The quality that maintains an alive relationship is service because service functions beyond time. The classic reasons for getting into a relationship are romance, money, power, youth and sex. All of these reasons are valid, but know that they will lose their attraction in time. Do not expect them to last. Just enjoy them and when they fade be thankful for having experienced them. Beware especially of clinging to them. Service, in simple terms, is "taking care of each other." Service is support and functions beyond reasons and time. We value service most during rough times, but our mistake is that we take it for granted the rest of the time. It is healthy to take time to notice those who serve us and regularly acknowledge their contributions. What is of ultimate value in your relationships is service.

- Recognize that service is the only reason that lasts, the only binding clause of a long-lived relationship.
- Learn that it is service that gives any relationship its true value.
- Know that all other reasons will not last. Reasons transform as you transform and your partners transform.

And when all of those reasons begin to fall away or dissipate, notice how you feel. If you are upset or feel jilted and angry, you are holding onto something that is no longer there. Be thankful that you had it for the time you did with that person. And if you truly served each other you will always remain friends.

Be sure that service and the acknowledgment of service is present in all of the relationships you value. The act of acknowledgment transforms your experience of yourself and your relationships. The simple act of acknowledging your mother and father as your origin, your source of life and aliveness, makes you more alive. They gave you the greatest gift you have: your aliveness and your ability to see, smell, taste, touch, feel and think.

The act of acknowledgment is the secret to progress. Once you acknowledge where you are you are no longer there. The nature of acknowledgement is to move forward. The faster you move forward, the more alive your relationships become. Once you acknowledge your mother and father as your creators then you may experience them as dear old friends rather than continuing to act like parents.

One of the obvious motives to become involved in a relationship is to experience satisfaction. The conscious act of serving is the obvious opportunity for creating such satisfaction. Serving someone becomes the opportunity to:

- Give.
- Contribute.
- Encourage.
- Represent.
- Assist.
- Support.
- Nourish.
- Approve.
- And acknowledge all of the above.

In relationships many of us become trapped in our limiting, unconscious conditioning. We miss the opportunity to experience satisfaction because, through unconscious conditioning, we experience service as servile.

For those caught in that dilemma service is: to work for someone else, to have duties, to be obedient, to be used or having to perform for someone else. When you become aware that consciously serving others creates satisfaction, contentment and pleasure it will and you will experience all of those things. From that moment you will never take service for granted or allow service to go unnoticed.

When service, however, is based on past negative beliefs and experiences it creates the following results in your relationships:

- You feel beneath people and not capable of a peer relationship.
- You experience yourself as only worthy of working for someone rather than with someone.
- You generally do not respect, love or admire those for whom you work.
- You are resentful of duties rather than experiencing them as chosen responsibilities.
- You are fearfully obedient rather than willing to be supportive.
- You perform for family, friends and business colleagues constantly, pretending to be who you think they want you to be rather than willing to risk being accepted for who you are.
- You serve people in authority because you live in fear of their control and power over you rather than being around and studying with them out of choice.
- You are deficiency motivated rather than growth motivated.
- You serve at the level of just being sufficient, never experiencing being good enough or great.
- You generally maintain and defend rather than open yourself to experience and growth.

Experiencing service through old beliefs eventually creates isolation, scarcity, separateness, boredom, burnout and the obvious ultimate dissatisfaction: eventually service becomes suffering. When you experience service consciously in present time the results in your relationships are very different:

- You contribute to the lives of others and therefore yourself.

- You assist people, knowing that they are capable, lovable and generous; you reassure them so that they can experience themselves in the same way.
- You support people who pursue the highest purpose in their lives even when they are unaware of their own ability.
- You encourage the people you serve to live, take risks and become free, even when their choices differ from yours.
- You nourish and share what you have, knowing there is great abundance.
- You serve people, as they choose to have you represent them, when you understand that your service to them is an extension of who they are.
- You're willing to give because you realize that what you give has been given to you.
- You accompany and are a companion to those whom you serve.
- You improve and correct without needing the approval of those you serve.
- You approve of those you serve.
- You forgive those you serve.
- Through service you experience peak experiences. Be aware and serve someone now.

Remember all other reasons for a relationship will transform as you transform. So, consider:

- If your relationship is a source of financial security, what will you do when you are self-sufficient?
- If you "fall in love," what will you do if you "fall out of love"?
- If your relationship is about money, sex, status, fame, power, family or knowledge then understand that all of these reasons will transform.

You have had wants and desires since the day you were born and you always will. Just be aware of what you are really willing to have. Take care, be conscious of the long-range value of service, and serve in your relationships. Here are some basics to ensure a satisfying relationship:

- Stop giving and denying. Start serving and receiving.
- Create a satisfying relationship with yourself before you expect satisfaction from others.
- Remember, "falling in love" is not a valid basis for a relationship. Service is.
- Stop "falling in love." Instead accept and communicate the meaning of "I love you" as: "You have served me by getting me in touch with the lovable, capable me who chooses to love you now."
- Always acknowledge and communicate your gratitude for the contributions and service of others in your life.

∞

Quality 6

Trust and Affinity

Throughout my life I have been continuously traveling, always transforming, and I have learned to trust. The willingness to reach out to someone is essential. I share this lifetime with those I choose, which makes trusting simple. And I always trust until there is a reason not to trust. What is the alternative? To be fearful? To be a skeptic? Trust is about whatever you are doing at the moment. It is about feeling an affinity with wherever you are and whomever you are with.

Affinity has become simple for me. I always feel it immediately and when it is strong and true I trust I know the people like we have shared life before. Our relationships usually have some bearing on what we do in the present and often there is nothing to do but love each other and be complete. Nothing to heal, nothing to create, just to be – that is true affinity.

Trust: Is to consciously doubt, as opposed to unconsciously doubt, in a relationship. Conscious doubt stems from the continuous transformation of doubt to trust in that relationship.

Affinity: The occupation of the same idea or thought. To like or to love someone, which implies agreement.

Integrity: The state of being complete, honest and sincere because of the integration of your chosen values and behavior.

There are many reasons why we lack the experience of trust in our relationships. We tend to create so many rules and expectations, both communicated and withheld, that it is a no-win game for whoever is in relationship with us. With excessive expectations any action in accordance with one's own rules usually violates the other's rules. Another reason for doubt and distrust in our relationships is that most of us have no conscious experience of how trust is created.

In our society most people are more comfortable with "blind faith" in relationships than the conscious creation of trust. The experience of trust comes with the realization that doubt transforms to trust either in the external, which fulfills your expectation, or in yourself who doubted for good reason. Your doubts should be expressed and shared rather than withheld in fear or shame. When they are shared discomfort usually occurs, but then you will notice that you and your relationship are moving to a deeper level of trust and satisfaction.

Trust is the context for a long-term relationship because long-term intimacy occurs. Trust is essential to intimacy because intimacy is impossible without taking risk. As you are already aware, at times intimacy may hurt. By its nature, being intimate means:

- Being visible.
- Being vulnerable.
- Risking rejection.
- Discovering freedom.
- Touching, forgiving and being honest.

Intimacy is neither safe nor easy, but without trust, intimacy does not occur. Trust is also essential to the aliveness in relationships because it creates the willingness to risk and to correct mistakes. Self-trust or "your truth" allows you to be intimate at will with whomever you choose. When this state of consciousness is achieved it allows us to re-experience the safety, security, sense of peace and satisfaction we felt as an infant in our mother's arms.

Trust also creates affinity, which is the liking or loving of another human being. This implies agreement and the occupation of the same idea or thought. Affinity and trust are essential and provide the opportunity for all healing in relationships. Trust put into action becomes integrity, the state of being whole.

Being aware of your doubts and know that going into them consciously transforms them into self-trust. At times all of us have had thoughts such as:

- "Don't get too deeply involved with love; it might not last; you might get hurt."
- "Do not show your true feelings; no one will love you how you truly are, they'll go away."
- "You need lots of money to feel secure, but if you have lots of money, someone will take it from you; or love you only because you have money."

With consciousness, and the willingness to experience each of these thoughts and other doubts, you transform into higher doubts until you are capable of the ultimate doubt called trust, which is truth. The way to truly trust is to doubt. Do not repress your doubts at any point, otherwise you will mistrust. Trust comes out of doubt, not by repressing, but by experiencing it to the ultimate. Doubt and trust are inseparable. They are polarities of the same experience, which is truth, your truth.

In time you will trust because it is more fun and contributes to your aliveness. Your trust then is a choice over doubt, an awareness of a more rewarding state called trusting. If you avoid doubt then you avoid yourself. You cannot arrive at the experience of self-trust this way. Instead, you will rely on beliefs and faith, living the truths of others instead of achieving your own.

Trust is also a present-time phenomenon. Understanding this means that you can say:

- "Everything is OK the way it is," rather than, "Everything will be OK."
- You say, "I trust you," rather than ask, "Will you trust me in the future?"

With this awareness, you can observe doubt in yourself and others.

- You do not identify with doubt.
- You are not disturbed by doubt.
- Doubt is there and you are watching it; you are not it.

In fact, you realize your doubt is the doorway to new discoveries and new experiences. Doubt is the origin of creative greatness. Doubt is the essential ingredient to achieving trust because it is an instinct, a perception. Don't be ashamed to doubt. Doubt does not mean you are making others wrong. It means you have work to do. Doubt means you need to explore and communicate it.

- Don't doubt the doubt. Trust doubt. You are coming from a place of knowing.
- Don't ignore doubt. Examine doubt and become clear about what you doubt.
- Don't distrust doubt. Trust yourself.

Doubt is not skepticism. Skeptics and cynics are constantly looking for what is wrong and are busy setting themselves up to be victims.

We don't know enough to be skeptics. In terms of the evolution of our consciousness, we have only appeared moments ago. In relationship to our planet, we are the new kids on the block.

When you have become one who trusts, you are alive, natural and spontaneous. You easily move into the unknown becoming more and more alive and more like yourself. Ultimately, your intelligence will allow you to distinguish the difference between trust and faith, the difference between your truth and the truths of others. Those who are unconscious have unconscious relationships. They require faith.

- Anytime you trust anything other than yourself or your experiences you are dealing with faith.
- Faith is buying into someone else's dogma. It can be a good first step but, if you rely on faith, you will lose trust in yourself.

People who are unconscious need emotional and sentimental promises from their partners and leaders. These are borrowed experiences. They substitute faith for credibility. Trust, however, is a present-time phenomenon. It is only true in present time and so not transferable. If you are asked if you will trust someone later, you can either say, "I don't know" or you can lie. When you begin to live your own truth you are gaining ground, but you won't arrive at self-trust as long as you continue to live by the rules and restrictions of others. You will not experience yourself as original, which is what you are. "Alive" people:

- Are intelligent.
- View their self as original.
- Trust their own experience acquired by their own authority.
- Are in alive relationships.
- Are authentic and exude confidence.
- Willing to transform personally.

- Recognize security is the ability to adapt and transform.
- Trust the essential ingredient to creativity.
- Know that creativity is impossible unless you are willing to destroy what you already have.
- Are willing to experience and to risk making their doubts known.
- Willing to "do it the wrong way" rather than to do it the way everyone else is doing it.

Self-trust has always been the key to greatness. What makes heroines like Joan of Arc great was not that she had spiritual visions, but that she dared to trust herself and her inner self. Every great leader or inventor is faced with detractors, ridicule and scorn because what they propose challenges the accepted norm. Self-trust is required of those who are willing to transform the ordinary into the extraordinary. Self-trust is an essential ingredient in all of your relationships. It allows you to feel the ecstasy of experiencing, "I really did that well."

∞

Quality 7

Effective Communication

Communication is the key to everything. My seminars and courses are successful because they are communicated effectively. That's the intention and why they were created. People choose to return because they had an extraordinary experience and learned something useful in their lives. What makes a seminar or program effective is the ability of the leader to engender direct experience and to create thoughts in others. Every day I see people who are literally dying because of their inability to communicate. They are dying to create. And life is a creative experience.

Effective communication: The interchange of ideas between two points, causing the re-creation of someone else's experience intentionally.

Effective communication:

- Dissolves feelings of separateness.
- Clears up misunderstandings, conflicts and resentments.
- Transforms relationships.

Alive relationships have stated directions and goals and, when these are consciously communicated and accomplished, they transform into new goals and directions to be communicated and accomplished.

- Effective communication creates harmony. Harmony is accuracy without struggle or effort. Effective communication creates clarity.

- Clarity is a high state of being able to cause, knowingly, whatever you are willing to have.

When you do not have clarity about what you are willing to communicate, you will have what someone else wants. Clarity is not a vague picture. Clarity is specific. If you do not have clarity you will create other people's results and eventually resent both the results and the people with whom you are communicating. There is a popular misconception that if you have clarity about something you have to stick with it forever. With clarity, however, you are also clear that you have the right to change. And to change you have to make a new choice, communicate it, change direction and create it. When you are clear about a relationship you will create it, which means that the relationships you have you are creating, either consciously or unconsciously.

When you combine common goals, harmony and clarity you receive agreement. Agreement is reality, as we know it. When your family is in agreement it will do whatever it is your family agrees to do. Clarity is having an image of what you are willing to have and getting people to agree with that image. When you are in an alive relationship you have agreement. In the course of that relationship when you have a disagreement you need a new agreement. The process, often subtle, of creating new agreements creates a new relationship. It probably won't look the same, but you are still in the relationship. When agreements change you may also experience upset, a refusal to communicate, a walking away and "not being" in a relationship, which is really still a relationship it's just a dead one.

Effective communication eliminates withholds, which are unexpressed positive or negative thoughts. Withholds absolutely drain your aliveness. They create disease. Withholds are:

- The point from which you are experiencing. They are only your opinions.
- They lack of self-expression, which is death.
- The experience of not allowing others to discover something about you.
- Reducing your relationships to things.
- Cause you to experience your relationships as threatening.
- Positive withholds kill as effectively as negative ones. When you are incapable of telling someone you love them, or of telling someone how valuable they are in your life, you are withholding and effectively destroying them and yourself.

Alternately, expressing your withholds empowers others to re-create you, to agree with you, to know you and to love you. Most of us communicate at the level of exchanging "our" opinions, beliefs or points of view. This entire matrix for communication is deficiency motivated, because "my point of view" vs. "your point of view" becomes "my fact" vs. "your fact." The truth is, there are no facts, only experience. Experience is the uniqueness of your participation in anything.

Communication is something that we inherit. Most of us communicate the way it was modeled for us, which is rarely described as effective. My former wife and I came from two diametrically opposed communication matrices: she came from the northern European "tight-lipped" style and I came from the loud, arm-waving southern Mediterranean style. While these contrasts created some great drama, which is frequently confused for communication, little was communicated effectively.

Effective communication is:

- A skill, a learned art, a science.
- What happens when you are willing to intentionally re-create and duplicate another person's experience.
- Effort and struggle disappear because you are willing to drop your point of view and become the person with whom you are communicating.
- The expression of your full intention.

Intention is the creative assertion of your purpose, and expressing your intention effectively is 90 percent of effective communication. Intention is that quality which brings anything into being. Expressing intention:

- On the physical plane is energy capable of creating and destroying matter.
- The first step in the process of effective communication.
- Sets off the spontaneous chain reaction of ideas, which is intentional communication.
- Brings experience into being.
- Has nothing to do with wanting or feelings, for which it is often confused, and everything to do with willingness.

Effective communication requires the constant discipline of expressing intention. And you can only demand full attention from someone when your intention is clear. Expressing intention is commonly experienced as negative, rude or unnecessary because most people communicate from a matrix of being covertly nice. When communication is intentional you transcend your limits and all reactive thought disappears. Talking about your intentions is like talking about sex. There is an absence of action and therefore an absence of satisfaction. Alive relationship happens when you realize your intention and make it true in the world.

Effective communication will not occur with something or someone:

- For whom you have no affinity.
- With whom you are unwilling to agree and for whom you do not intend to change.

These three factors must be present for an alive relationship to occur:

- Affinity, which is the occupation of the same idea or concept. It is the degree of love or liking for someone or something.
- Agreement is consent to a course of action. The degree of agreement reached by both communicators determines the reality, therefore, that which is real is real simply because it is agreed upon.
- The universal and essential ingredient to all communication is relationship in which change is recognized and valued. Without relationship, no communication can occur.

The most common limit to effective communication is the continuous chatter that runs on and on in your brain. When you are willing to risk expression in life the chatter is reduced, and sometimes even eliminated, and you experience brief moments of clarity. The amount of brain chatter is the difference between:

- An unconscious person and a conscious person.
- A common communicator and an effective communicator.
- An unenlightened being and an enlightened being.

The total absence of brain talk is true in the "now" as creative, causal communication occurs in the moment and not in the past. Creative communication occurs when we are willing:

- To express intention.
- To create.
- To be absent of vested interest and the need to be right.
- To give our attention.
- To re-create or duplicate.
- Have a thought, belief, opinion or point of view we are willing to release.

A major pitfall in communication is the belief that if your words did not get through the first time, you should "say it again." Words are just words and do not create compliance, understanding or creation. Communicating at the level of choice vs. decision requires you to be able to make a distinction between:

- Choice: A selection made freely. Choice is intuitive. It is deliberate. Choice comes from you for reasons known or unknown. It is freedom in that moment that is absent of reasons.
- Decision: Has reasons and is predetermined. Reason comes from outside of you, from considering others, and entails responsibility and obligation.

To communicate effectively, you must first become aware of your communication matrix. The following is an example of what most of us do in our communication and must change to be effective: A young couple is walking down a shopping street. They pass a music store playing a song the man's mother sang to him as a child. Instead of enjoying the sweep of nostalgia the man is moved to ask his friend to marry him. He could have just bought the record.

When you set up your matrix for communication you set up your life to happen within this context. Whatever you result in your life is not possible unless it happens within your matrix. Eventually your life looks just like more of the same because you create only results that can happen within your matrix. It's important to effective communication that you know where you are coming from and see how your points of view confine you. When you communicate from a point of view you will look for and create evidence to prove that point of view. When you sit inside your matrix and constantly communicate to make yourself right you make everyone else wrong.

To communicate effectively you need to look at the way you know about communication – not what you know but rather the way you know it. The way you know about something is the way you remember it and store it. Stored information has nothing to do with communication. It has to do with the survival of your points of view. Events in our lives actually occur in a linear series of "now" moments, but we do not store these events in a linear form. Instead, we arrange them in the form of concepts, beliefs and groups of memories. These become systems of evidence by which we support our points of view and eliminate others.

When you say, "I know what you are saying," what you are really saying is, "I have a memory of what you are saying." When you say, "I understand you," what you are really saying is, "Your system of beliefs and mine agree." What you call "perception" is actually what you already know and have stored in your organized memory or matrix. When you are in an alive relationship insights occur more often. Insights are what happen when:

- You are outside your system or matrix and you are in someone else's for the first time.

- When you are out of your brain and accessing mind. One beneficial insight to realize first is that the way you have it organized is what you see.

If you are to communicate creatively, you must be willing to reorganize what you think you know. It also helps to realize that an insight to you is always the memory of someone else's experience that is stored in the mind. When you ask someone to explain something what you are really saying is that you want him to restate it so that it fits your communication matrix.

Communicating emotions is easy once you accept that you create them. For example, to experience sadness, you must have a stored memory of happiness. Of course, what is sad to you may very well be happy to someone else. That is because sadness and happiness are both concepts and not real. They are expressed that way because that's the way the individuals expressing those emotions have them stored. It's "their" experience of sadness and happiness. Hungry to me is not hungry to someone else. When you receive this insight, you become joyous because you realize that you don't have to be happy all of the time, which may make you very happy. People often think I'm not happy because I'm deep in thought and not smiling. What's true for me is that I'm very happy most of the time simply peacefully witnessing existence.

Eventually we learn that:

- Resisting an emotion is what keeps you in the emotion.
- Expressing an emotion dissolves the emotion and it transforms.

When you are communicating effectively you are moving from misunderstanding toward compassion. Misunderstanding occurs when someone is communicating with you and instead of receiving the communication you react from memory. Your memory has nothing to do with what is being communicated. Misunderstanding is created when a friend says, "I really loved the beach today," and you say, "I hate the beach." Your friend did not say, "You really loved the beach today." With your response, you didn't recreate their experience. You just dredged up your own. Misunderstanding occurs when communication is absent of compassion. Communicating through compassion is what creates miracles in people and it is what gets you past the forms of things and people. With it, you realize the value of what is being shared and create alive relationships.

- Compassion is your knowing another's contribution.
- Compassion is the conscious re-creation of what someone else is giving up. It's the re-creation of their experience.
- Compassion is to be with another being totally, to receive wit out judgment their experience and to re-create it.
- Compassion gives you the knowledge needed to serve another.

Effective communication:

- Resolves problems and dissolves feelings of separateness.
- Clears misunderstandings, memory of experience, conflicts and resentment.
- Transforms individuals and groups into a team with a common goal.

Effective communication creates:

- Harmony: Accuracy and efficiency with less effort and struggle.
- Clarity: A high state of being able to cause knowingly.
- Reality: The degree of agreement reached by both communicators. That which is real is real simply because it is agreed.

- Affinity: The relative distance and similarity of the two communicators. It implies the occupation of the same idea.
- Results: Anything as it is, absent of point of view and personality.
- Consciousness: Aliveness and life, existing as both ability and state, and usually attributed to "living" organisms (plant and animal). In my experience, consciousness is present in everything.
- Consciousness as ability: The attribute of certain living organisms, which enables them to be aware. It is the phenomenon of thought itself, of awareness, perception, imagination and emotion.
- Consciousness as awareness: The ability of an organism to perceive and to sense its own existence.

Withheld communications is: Undisclosed information about an individual or group, which causes you to be threatened.

Withheld communication creates:

- Placement of individuals and groups in survival-threatening situations.
- Covert thought and behavior, individuals and groups are less powerful, less effective, less joyful and less loving.
- A communication lag. Individuals and groups are out of present time and therefore not in communication with themselves or their environment. This is death.
- Creates elation and depression, the highs and lows that occur when an individual is connected to a suppressive person, group, thought or behavior pattern. Suppressed communication must be effectively communicated continuously to transform the individual and/or group into an alive relationship.

Failure to communicate is:

- A general unwillingness to duplicate or to "be."
- Unwillingness to express intention, the act that brings experience into being.
- Unwillingness to receive or recreate, not to allow into your experience what is already there.
- Unwillingness to re-create, occupy copy and be alive.
- Unwillingness to experience distance.
- Unwillingness to change, destroy, create, let go or become a creator.
- Unwillingness to give attention, an act possible only with clear intention.
- Unwillingness to acknowledge and understand or to make known publicly that you have received the communication.

Effective communication breaks down:

- When you're trying to make yourself right.
- When inappropriate emotion is attached to communication.
- When the wrong context or content exists.

Effective communication is: What happens when we give up the struggle to communicate.

∞

Quality 8

Absence of Parental Authority

Most of us experience authority as control. When superiors are viewed as controlling bosses there is distrust. But another form of authority exists, which is absolutely precise and effective when you experience others as teachers from whom you have chosen to learn. True authority is respected. You communicate to true authority and value the opportunity to apprentice with true authority.

Authority: Someone or something you choose to be influenced by and learn from.

Two characteristics vital to an alive relationship are honesty and the absence of guilt. What is often overlooked is that it is impossible to lie or to experience guilt in the absence of authority as most people experience it. If you are being dishonest in any one of your relationships, you need to look at how much power you have given that relationship.

If you are dishonest about how much money you make, look at how much power you have given money and what it symbolizes to you. If you are lying to your wife, your husband, or someone else close to you, consider how much control and power you have given that person.

If you are lying to your parents, discover that you have outgrown your parents. If you still relate to your mother and father as parents, as authorities, you are stuck in time and you must create a new alive relationship with them, absent of control and need for their validation.

There is no such thing as dishonesty when you are not accountable to anybody.

Guilt is not a feeling. It is a form of manipulation. It is a device used by people to control others. It is used to get others to do what those in authority want them to do. Parents effectively use guilt to control their children, and eventually children use it to control their parents. When you are self-determined guilt does not exist. Despite popular belief children do not learn to lie from lower socioeconomic groups in schoolyards. Children learn to lie for their survival. In order to protect themselves, and those they love, they learn to lie through interactions with parents and other authority figures.

Your father or mother asks you to tell the truth about your childhood adventures; you do and you are punished. A friend asks what you think of his girl friend; you respond honestly and he chooses to abandon your friendship.

You learn early in life that truth hurts, especially those you love. In fact, you learn that love brings up a lot of other experiences unlike love, such as pain, rejection, control, fear, etc. You come home and mom says, "Johnny, where were you today?" You say, "Oh, nowhere, just out playing." She smiles, checks that you have two arms, hands, legs and eyes and that is all she really wants to know. And you now know that. You have created a matrix for relating to your loved ones dishonestly. And you continue to relate in that way in your adult relationships.

Parents ask you for the truth, and if you tell them the truth they make it clear to you that you have hurt them. Some even physically hurt you for having hurt them with the truth. You begin to lie because you love them and depend on them. Dishonesty, then, becomes a by-product of love. Be careful, because this becomes a behavior pattern which you then continue, with surrogate parents, spouses, your own children and everyone else you love. At the root of this behavior pattern is authority, some of which can be traced to your prenatal state. Since before you were born, significant others have been planning their dreams as your life. Therefore, you may appear to be hostile or rebellious when your life choices don't agree with their dreams. You have to be aware and consciously attentive to keep that kind of authority out of your life.

Everybody, it seems, wants to come into your life and tell you what to do. They have plans for you, which mean that from the time before you entered the world, you are one way or another, at the effect of authority. You come into the world with:

- A name.
- An ethnic heritage.
- A religious belief.
- A socioeconomic background.
- A particular gender.
- So, you are defined to death, a victim of "semanti-cide" or the killing of humans by definition.

People in alive relationships are themselves. They either experience an affinity for others or they don't. You know that they have that right, as you do. If you are in an alive relationship, you generally do not take opinions personally. That does not mean that you do not care about yourself and others. It just means that you are not willing to be for them something other than what you are. If they contribute to your life in a meaningful way, however, you will change effortlessly and out of choice. When you are in an alive relationship you like who you are. When you like and love who you are you do not need authority as control.

The degree to which you drop authority as control is directly proportional to the degree to which you nurture yourself and others, as well as create results in your life. When authority is control you come to depend on it, you literally stop growing, and you stop the life process itself.

An alive relationship cannot exist in a dishonest environment. Honesty is the soil in which aliveness blooms. The irony of this is that while an alive relationship cannot survive a dishonest relationship, the romance that brought you together will not survive an honest one. So you have to make a choice between love and romance, between honesty and dishonesty. The choice should be clear. At some point in life, if you are to grow in your relationship, you must choose between alive relationship and romance.

When the romance begins to fall away and you start relating at a different level, you may get an uneasy feeling based on your belief systems and society's constant hammering away at its obsession with romance that something is wrong. Should honesty prevail, however, nothing is wrong; it is just time to move to a higher level, a level of service and taking care of one another. As the romance fades and the relationship becomes something other than "heat" it moves into a level of compensation called compassionate love. At this level you don't need or want the illusion of romance because you are consciously loving and being consciously loved by choice.

Romance as a significant ingredient fades away because it is a less gratifying experience. It is not unlike our early craving for refined sugar, which for most of us diminishes as we become more aware of other, more subtle and satisfying choices. As love cannot survive a dishonest relationship, the steam of romance will evaporate in an honest relationship. You begin to look at romance with the healthy respect you have for an occasional holiday. If you need romance within the context of such a relationship, be creative. Create a little positive drama. You can always spice it up a bit and just enjoy the romance knowing that it is an illusion, a vacation from which you will return home to compassionate love.

Although a relationship can obviously occur in a dishonest environment, it will not survive. Within the accepted structure of our competitive society, many people do business or parent their children dishonestly and consider it shrewd. They take pride in their cunning ways and tactics. But these proud actions will kill a loving relationship. To survive and to flourish a loving relationship cannot survive and will die in the absence of honesty.

Courage is required to be honest. It takes guts. It requires you to be comfortable with yourself. The old saying, "Honesty is the best policy," really does not describe the quality of honesty I'm talking about. The quality I'm describing is more spiritual and more an affair of the heart. Once honesty is "a policy," it is a political and change-resistant form of manipulation – something you use to gain something. Honesty at this level ceases to be wise or intelligent. It is control. Those who are conscious and intelligent people have no interest in being a controlling authority. They realize that being domineering creates short-term relationships and they are more interested in loving people and knowing themselves. Consider:

- When you love yourself, you don't want to escape yourself.
- If you control or dominate another person, you are attempting to escape from yourself.

Being a domineering authority is one of the great escapes. It keeps you occupied day and night. You experience and think about control before you go to sleep, during sleep and the moment you wake up. To be in authority is a twenty-four-hour job. You are afraid to truly relax because if you do you will lose control. Honesty, in the absence of authority, bubbles to the top for the sheer joy of it. It's not there to gain anything. It creates freedom and joy. Without authority there is nothing to lose, so you are willing to lose everything. Honesty, without authority, is the courage to be your self. To be who you are and what you are. Since authority does not want you to be yourself, honesty can't exist within an authoritarian relationship.

We complain constantly about the abuse we experience in our authoritarian relationships. Such authority creates expectations toward and from our relationships. They pretend and we pretend. They promise and we promise. Then, if we escape such a relationship, we run into the cage of another only to realize that nothing has changed. But when we are freed from our early life of being conditioned by authority, we suddenly experience a freedom. We experience the joy of being honest and guilt free. We move from the policy that "It's always to your advantage to tell the truth" to the experience that "It's always to your advantage to tell yourself the truth."

Alive relationships don't need parental authority. This chapter and this book show you how to rediscover the intelligence with which you were born. Those who control you now, parents, spouse, children, employer, therapist, guru, etc., may not be comfortable with you reading this book, especially if it works for you and causes you to be honest and without the need for parental authority. Just keep in mind:

- Parental authority creates seriousness, not happiness.
- Parental authority creates division, not relatedness.

Face the fact that twenty to thirty years or more of parental authority have destroyed much of what was valuable in you. It has destroyed:

- Honesty.
- Joy.
- Freedom.
- Creativity.
- All the other gifts of your birth.

In exchange, you got the lies, theories, words, jargon and more words. The spontaneity and instincts of birth have been sacrificed for dead knowledge, reactions, obedience and duty.

Those of us who have chosen to be in alive relationships are seeing parental authority for what it is: hypnosis, a conditioning, molded by the brain. Authority as control is opposed to the expansion of consciousness. For example, when the spiritual teacher Krishnamurti was only a young boy, the theosophists wanted him to be a "world teacher." But he grew too intelligent for this. He knew there had never been a world teacher nor will there ever be a world teacher. But even with his intelligence, the scars of authority could be seen in him. Both his seriousness and his difficulty with humor were marks left by the theosophists.

To be in a relationship with an authoritarian person is to live in a desert. It is to be unconscious. It is to be with people that do not allow you to blossom, to flower, to grow, or, most destructive of all, to communicate. You say one thing and they hear something else. Your communication, hence your relationships, are filled with constant misinterpretations. When you talk, they hear their parents, their Sunday-school teacher and their collective discipline. However, when you are absent of authority:

- You talk and listen spontaneously and listen compassionately.
- Your relationships become existential, trusting and present.

Teaching your children or students without parental authority sounds more like sharing. Teachers in this environment resemble companions. They lose their authoritarian overtones. In this environment, students don't feel taught, but rather caught by choice. Intelligence, in truth, cannot be taught. Rather, it must be experienced and then acknowledged.

Alive relationships cannot be forced; ecstatic relationships cannot be enforced; intelligent people cannot long be regimented, ordered or commanded. Blatant authority does not appeal to understanding; it does not open the heart. It just says, "Do this. Do that." Once you lose your need for parental authority:

- You become self-determined.
- You become your own parent.
- You become an individual and you see individuals everywhere.
- You see faces for the first time, hear laughter and joy, feel excitement.
- Most of the time, you experience being loved.

Loving authority does not judge you or anyone else. It examines only your behavior. It means that your work, not you the person, is corrected. Loving authority when extended nourishes you and your work improves in the process. The absence of parental authority allows you to feel energy to move beyond the dichotomy of work and play. Without parental authority relationships create their own authority. A collective authority occurs. It is not forced. It is synchronized. Everyone plays a different instrument, but the harmony and the beat are together. An orchestra has a conductor, but the conductor is just another part of the whole in tune with the instruments. A flow occurs between the conductor and the orchestra. It is the same with alive relationships.

It is an environment in which the rigidity of "do this" and "do that" authority is no longer a pervasive presence. True authority will give you your knowledge, not its own. True authority creates intelligence, not imposing intellectuals. As an adult, you need nothing imposed on you.

∞

Quality 9

The Ability to Receive

All that you give and deny in your relationships will be given and denied to you. Giving and receiving are the source of true ecstasy of our relationships. This is what being alive is all about.

Receive: To allow into your reality what is already there, ecstasy in relationship. Alive relationships are about:

- Serving.
- Receiving.
- Creation.
- Re-creation.

As a newborn child you were not in a giving and denying relationship. You were in a giving and receiving relationship, which is commonly called unconditional love. Then, out of necessity, your mother and father became your parents. With that the rules came into play, because the job of parenting can be done only through the use of conditional love. You sometimes experienced parenting as your mother and father not loving you. At times, most likely they had a similar experience. If you have not yet forgiven your parents for this it is manifesting itself in your current relationships as disease. At some point, your parents began to:

- Give to you and deny you.
- Reward your proper performance.

- And appropriately prepare you to function in our society, which considers children to be misfits who must be trained.

As you grew older, more and more you assumed the role of either giver or denier. In ignorance, you may have chosen to fault one of these roles usually the denier. What's true is that these roles were assumed as children and were essential to our survival as children. Deniers were usually invaded, made to perform, berated or asked constant questions. As adults, they learned to protect rather than surrender. Deniers, in fact, are afraid of being:

- Overcome.
- Conquered.
- Smothered.
- Possessed.
- Weakened.
- Exploited.
- Invaded.

Givers, as children, experienced their childhood as being deprived of nurturing or attention. The actual conditions are unimportant. What is important is their "experience" of the conditions. Some were actually weaned early, not held or bonded or left alone much of the time. The giver, then, learns to:

- Please.
- Initiate.
- Seek.
- Manipulate.

Givers get to be the "good guys." Deniers get to be the "bad guys." Givers get little attention. Deniers get lots of attention. Givers have a tendency to feel:

- Turned on.
- Accepting.
- Sexual.
- Committed.
- Rejected.
- Wanting.
- Needy.
- Victimized.

Deniers have a tendency to feel:

- Disconnected.
- Critical.
- Neutered.
- Indecisive.
- Desired.
- Superior.
- Untouchable.
- Abusive.

The tendency now is to go again into your relationships unconsciously and to do exactly the same thing. You give and deny your relationships depending on whether you approve of their behavior or not. You are consciously or unconsciously parenting them. Givers see their partners as wrong and abusive. They are always "feeling the pain" of really being in love and then being rejected. Deniers see their partners as right, but misguided. They "feel guilty" for rejecting their partner's love, but they perceive themselves as unlovable.

What givers and deniers have in common is fear. The giver is afraid that if they stop giving no one will want them. The denier is afraid that if they stop denying no one will want them. This mutual fear in a relationship creates power struggles about sex, money, household, children – anything and everything. The giver begins to give to control and conquer. The denier begins to deny because they perceive their selves above the giver, has chosen beneath their selves and deserve better. Usually, under all that, what is true is that they feel unlovable. When givers and deniers have lost enough power struggles, they create distance by:

- Defining territory.
- Creating facades.
- Being involved with their work to the exclusion of their relationships or family.
- Being involved with their children or family to the exclusion of spouse or lover.

Eventually, they blame each other, creating distance and mutual isolation. In fact, many of us reach the point at which we are constantly denying our relationships and therefore ourselves. Intimacy disappears and separation occurs. To create intimacy, you must first learn to reverse these roles. Indeed, you must first have certainty that you want intimacy because intimacy involves more than most people are willing to have in their relationships.

It is fascinating that most of us cannot openly receive. All of us experienced ourselves as either being denied or exploited as children. Therefore, we create givers who give in order to control their relationships. We create deniers who deny and control the givers. Both are so fearful of being hurt that they do not know how to just give and they cannot receive graciously. When you give into control and denial what you are really saying is: "I want to get out of this relationship. I am incapable of intimacy and receiving."

Receiving is one of the main reasons for being in a relationship. It is the opportunity to be accepted and validated. It is also the opportunity to acquire, learn, experience and change. The above reasons for receiving are conscious. They are "on purpose." Unfortunately, most people are not "on purpose," conscious or even close to being fully realized. For the majority, their reasons for receiving are pointless, lacking in awareness and stuck in the past.

For them, receiving can involve an encounter, being possessed, submitting to another's wishes, having others inflict their lives on them, suffering and being affected by some other force. Simply, if you believe receiving creates dissatisfaction and discomfort, then it will, since believing is ultimately defining. In other words, receiving is satisfaction or dissatisfaction, pleasurable or painful, being discontented or being content.

Your definitions determine your experience. When receiving is based on past negative beliefs or definitions, the results or experiences are relatively predictable. You feel burdened by all that has been given to you. You feel obliged and obligated. You constantly feel pressured by everyone and everything. You are possessive and jealous and you selfishly hoard all that has been given to you. When you share you have an agenda and believe that all others do.

You find yourself constantly encountering those who give to you because you believe you are unworthy of their gifts. You easily submit to criticism. You often "feel less than" and you take things personally. You have great difficulty receiving graciously, and you feel inflicted when it occurs. You feel compelled to "pay back" because you experience receiving as undergoing some sort of test. In general, you experience life as a tedious existence, requiring suffering, a struggle in which you usually feel victimized. These experiences invariably create results such as:

- Isolation.
- Separateness.
- Scarcity.
- Boredom.
- Burnout.
- General dissatisfaction.

The purpose and reason for relating will dissolve and the willingness to create stops. When you experience receiving in present time you accept the contributions of others openly and graciously. You receive information the way it is rather than filtering it through past archaic belief systems. You acquire material and nonmaterial possessions and skills because they support who you are and who you are willing to be rather than what others think you are or who they want you to be.

You know the difference between direct experience and memory of experience. You frequently have direct experiences, living more in the moment, without memory and reaction. You are more capable of learning intuitively through instinct for the purpose of "transformation" rather than acquiring knowledge to accumulate more "information."

As you learn intuitively you come to know that transformation is creation and that you are willing to experience it. You are free and open to new experience before evaluating and judging. You are capable and actively relate to the people you choose to become. You enjoy and multiply all you have received while simultaneously giving it away. You re-create yourself in others and encourage others to re-create themselves in you. You do this intentionally and with integrity. You validate the experience others have of themselves and you insist that they validate yours. You are aware of your transformation.

Transforming the way you receive will move you past:

- Duty and struggle.
- Scarcity and poverty.
- Separation and alienation.
- Loneliness and pain.
- Incomplete relationships.
- Self-pity and doubt.
- Unworthiness.
- Boredom and anger.
- Feeling ignored and unappreciated.
- Being isolated.

Receiving now, in present time, creates:

- Choice vs. compromise.
- Creativity vs. imitation.
- Abundance vs. exertion for wealth.
- Whole compassionate relationships.
- Acknowledgment and validation.
- Acceptance and power.

∞

Quality 10

Self-Esteem

Self-esteem is self-love. When you love yourself you are able to effort-lessly love everyone around you. This natural love just overflows; you cannot contain it. It is ecstatic. Self-esteem at its highest level is not egotistical behavior. Self-esteem at its highest functioning is making contributions to the lives of others. Both egotists and people of high esteem can often appear unconsciously selfish. The difference is that egotistical people are actually hostile.

Self-esteem: The reputation we acquire with ourselves, our most profound and important judgment.

For example, say you have a Mercedes-Benz. It is an incredible automobile and you love driving it because it is comfortable and it supports you. That is self-esteem. Now, if you were to feel terrific in your Mercedes because you are parked next to a humble economy car – that is hostility. When you have high self-esteem, you are willing for everyone to have a Mercedes and you do not experience yourself as better. You want everyone to have it because you know that if they do it will just lift you up as you lift everyone up with you. That is the difference between egotism and self-esteem. The egotist has an invest-ment in scarcity. People with high self-esteem experience and live their lives consistent with abundance.

Low self-esteem creates avoidance because you cannot acquire or maintain anything that you experience as being more significant than you. If you experience anyone or anything as more valuable and more significant than your self you will probably not acquire it. And if you do acquire it the acquisition will be brief and unsustainable. For example, if you think money is more important than you, you will remain poor. Or you will worry about money for the rest of your life, no matter how much you have.

We have been told for thousands of years that God is within each of us, and yet we refuse to hear it because of the responsibility inherent in that distinction. So you remain a seeker for the rest of your life, never attaining your god self or spiritual satisfaction. A common malady of relationships is that you don't feel quite right about yourself as if there is something slightly wrong with you and you keep looking for that perfect person to make you feel whole and complete. But if you ever found that perfect person, what would such a perfect person want with you, a bundle of self-perceived imperfections? Instead of searching for the perfect person, your time is best spent discovering that perfect person within you. When you do discover that perfect person within then alive relationships are available to you.

When you attain a high level of self-esteem you experience the absence of need. Within that absence of need what you needed suddenly becomes manifested in your life. Absence of need creates abundance. I do not know why this happens. What I do know is that it is a universal law, which happens, so I use it whenever I am aware of it.

In an alive relationship, the absence of need creates numerous extraordinary relationships, whereas when you chase after relationships you cause them to react and to move away from you. Each time you move to a higher level of self-esteem, you experience all your relationships as perfect and you know that only your definitions are wrong or outdated. With high self-esteem you know that what you have to work through are your definitions and perceptions and not your relationships. If you are egotistical you will work on your relationships; you will "get her to change" or you will "fix him." If you have a high level of self-esteem, you look at your relationships and say, "It is perfect the way it is, and it is not what I want." Or you choose to say, "It is perfect the way it is, but I am redefining what I want from the relationship," and you remain with the same person within a new context of relationship.

Self-esteem translated from the vernacular of "psycho-babble" is "love yourself." To move in the direction of higher self-esteem, you must accept yourself. This does not mean just saying "Okay," when someone asks, "How are you?" But rather accepting yourself so completely that you are willing to act on it, to actually be the way you are. The secret of effortless momentum toward higher self-esteem is the knowledge that we grow each time we accept ourselves and that each time we realize who we are we are not anymore. In order to begin to accept your self you must:

- Participate in life rather than be a spectator.
- Be conscious and aware without losing your personality.
- Be more spontaneous.
- Be emotionally and intellectually honest with yourself.
- Be willing to comprehend and enjoy interpersonal relationships.
- Risk living life fully while accepting you do not have to understand it fully.
- Be willing to share and experience the gifts and possessions of others without regretting that you do not possess them yourself.
- Risk not being guided by dogma and morals, allowing others their right to choose freely.
- Be willing to move toward your higher self without complete knowledge of what or who that is.
- Drop deficiency motivation. Be courageous and express your aliveness.

Self-trust is also essential to acquiring self-esteem. We have been exposed to so much constant negative feedback that we are basically irrational and destructive to others and ourselves. We must look deeper and discover the loving supportive self that lies buried beneath all this propaganda. When we do not look for the deeper truth we begin to believe that the negative propaganda is true. We begin to see negativity everywhere so we eventually believe that this disease lies within us. Fear and dread causes us to become doomsayers and cynics. The self-trust test is simple and requires only asking and answering the question, "Am I living in a way that is satisfying to me and that expresses me?"

The greatest gift a parent can give a child is a strong sense of self-worth. The most active way that you can contribute to the self-esteem of others and yourself is by validation and affirmation. Each time you threaten someone unnecessarily, callously reject someone, hurt or attempt to dominate another human being you are destroying self-esteem. Each time you are compassionate, supportive, sincere, affectionate and forgiving you are creating self-esteem.

When he was about four my son took charge of the situation when, with crayons and paper in hand, he said, "Listen Dad, I'll draw these pictures, hand them to you, and then you say "Great!"

Be aware that, without exception, every act against yourself or another, every departure from your higher self and true nature and purpose, every evil act or thought records itself in your unconscious mind and eventually these acts will cause you to despise yourself. Once you despise yourself sufficiently you will begin to discount yourself and when someone says, "You are a beautiful woman," and your insecure self says, "You haven't seen me without makeup." Or someone says, "You have a lovely smile," and your negatively conditioned self says, "You haven't seen me angry." And on it goes: "You're very intelligent."

is countered with "Yeah, but I'm not attractive." Non-affirmation is often less obvious. You negate the affirmation by qualifying it. Someone says, "That's a beautiful blouse you're wearing," and you respond with, "Yes, I got it on sale," or "Yes, I've had it for years." or you simply shrug your shoulders with no verbal response so the affirmation rolls off without your acceptance or acknowledgement.

Sometimes you avoid affirmation by giving immediate reciprocation. For example, you hear, "That's a fantastic shirt," and you respond, "Yes, I love yours, too." The classic covert way of avoiding receiving affirmation is to say to your self, "These people don't really know me so their validations are meaningless." Your inability to receive self-affirmation separates you from your experience of the way things are. Eventually you do not know yourself. And if you don't know yourself, you most assuredly cannot love yourself. Self-respect is another major contributor to self-esteem. It is an acquired skill and it increases with time if as with any acquired skill you follow certain basic guidelines.

The rules of self-respect are:

- You stop making yourself wrong when things don't go your way.
- Give yourself permission to grow, change and become whatever you choose.
- Exercise your right to privacy and to keep certain parts of your life secret.
- Accept that you have a right to be loved and to love others, to be cared for, fulfilled and even adored.
- You have the right to know and to ask questions of anyone at any time on any matter that affects your life.
- Your self-respect is implicit as long as you hurt no one else in acquiring it.

- You communicate your willingness to be happy and to have a purpose. This willingness is important even if it's without significance to others as long as it's rewarding to you.
- You practice trusting and being trusted.
- You are willing to be free and open to experience.
- You realize your right to win and lose, to succeed and fail, and to become whomever you choose to become.

Self-esteem is also enhanced by your ability to nourish yourself. Most of us stopped receiving our necessary nourishment when our mothers began transforming that role into one of parenting. To reactivate the experience of feeling nourished:

- Take the initiative to do whatever is necessary to get what you need. Do this rather than waiting and hoping that somehow, someone will give you what you need.
- Choose what is important to you. Do this rather than allowing others to make decisions for you.
- Be willing to take risks and to experience activities that create greater satisfaction in your life. Do this rather than clinging to old behavior patterns that offer the illusion of security.
- Focus on present time and what you are doing here and now. Do this rather than constantly wandering into the future and past and avoiding being present.
- Be the author determining your own life-style. Do this rather than allowing others to make you an extra in their movies. At least insist on being a co-star.
- Assume total responsibility for satisfying your own needs and desires. Do this rather than trying to manipulate others into satisfying you.
- Live your personal life as you choose and expect that there will usually be people who reject you for this choice. Do this rather than going through life explaining and seeking others approval.

- Start looking at what is exciting, adventurous and stimulating about your life. Do this rather than trying to survive life and experiencing life as a struggle.
- See life as a direction you are moving allowing yourself to grow until the day you die. Do this rather than creating cutoff points related to age, which cause you to dissipate new opportunities.
- Take responsibility for your conflicts and problems. Do this rather than projecting them onto others or blaming and playing victim.
- Become more self-determined by basing your behavior on your own experience. Do this rather than clinging to attitudes and old beliefs instilled in childhood.
- First accept yourself as you are, unless you choose to change. Do this rather than believing you must change to be accepted.
- Experience your mistakes as an integral part of learning. Do this rather than attacking and ridiculing yourself or going into disgust or self-denial when things don't go the way you want.
- Practice enlightened self-interest as an expression of the true you. Do this rather than believing selfishness is evil or bad.
- Know that nourishing yourself and others allows you to be cared for while being your own source of wellbeing. Do this rather than experiencing it as duty, desperate need or surrender of power.

The belief that selfishness is evil or negative behavior is the belief that has caused the decline of self-esteem in your reputation with yourself. The dichotomy between selfishness and unselfishness disappears in conscious healthy people. Duty cannot be distinguished from pleasure. Work blends with play. The most socially visible are also the most individualistic people. The most mature are often childlike. The most ethical frequently enjoy lust.

If you sacrifice everyday things to give your child an education, are you selfish or unselfish? Who receives the reward? Who gets the pleasure, you or your child? The rationalization for telling someone, "Don't be selfish" becomes "Don't be egotistical, inconsiderate or without concern for others." But unfortunately, "Don't be selfish" implies much more. It implies, "Don't do what you want to do. Do what I want you to do." This is a powerful form of manipulation camouflaged in ethics. It implies, "Give up your power to others; surrender yourself." Telling someone, "Don't be selfish" kills their self-esteem.

"Don't be selfish" is the most powerful tool for suppressing spontaneity. It stops the free development of personality. It has become an ethical way to ask people to sacrifice and submit. Self-esteem means to love yourself and loving yourself is your natural birthright. You can reclaim that vital quality by practicing the very act of loving yourself now. Never forget that we were all born with the birthright of self-esteem. Be mindful that this is also true of those born today. Remember:

- When children are exposed to undo criticism they will learn to condemn themselves and others.
- When children are treated with hostility they will learn to fight and to hurt themselves and others.
- When children are ridiculed and humiliated they will be shy and frightened and they will withhold.
- When children are taught to experience shame they will inflict guilt on themselves and others.
- When children are encouraged they will learn to be self-determined and to experience confidence in themselves and others.
- When children live with praise and validation they will appreciate themselves and others.

- When children are accepted and given approval they feel affinity for themselves; they like themselves and others.
- And when children are loved they will not only love themselves they will manifest self-esteem in others.

∞

Quality 11

Honorable Sexuality

When you accept your sexuality as honorable you experience yourself as whole, authentic and complete. Sex is a highly unique level of communication that joins people and allows them to leave their bodies. During orgasm we transcend our own body as well as our partner's body. We transcend biology. We experience a formless, metaphysical aliveness. We experience a level of conscious communication uncommon to everyday life. Unfortunately, the more common experience is pain, guilt and condemnation. Sex is an act during which the risk of intimacy just happens. It is an act with which we either feel satisfied or unsatisfied, competent or incompetent, and, most importantly, honored or humiliated.

Honorable sexuality: To experience doing only what satisfies you and your partner and honors you. This creates self-respect based on your self-determined values and ethics. Consequently, inherited mores and standards lose their power over you. To deny your sexuality is:

- To deny your very existence.
- To deny the act which created your aliveness.
- To deny what allows you to think, feel, see, smell, hear, and taste.
- And to simply deny everything as you now know it.

Honorable sex is really adult play. It is the opportunity for you to play with someone's body and to allow that person to play with yours. It enables you to be held, to experience the forgotten language of touch, to share, to express emotions, to laugh with each other, to share secrets, to be vulnerable, to be validated and to be honored. Achieving honorable sex is simple. Do only what you are willing to do with whom you choose. Do only what lifts you to a growing sense of self-confidence and respect and when you do anything short of that, notice it, accept it and move on. Just realize that honorable sexuality has nothing to do with form or preference, or anything other than you being okay about you.

Although the traditional male and female sexual attitudes and roles are disappearing it is evident that these roles have crippled men and women for centuries. They have made us guilty. They have made us prisoners. They have condemned sex, our most beautiful form of communication. Now the roles, standards and attitudes of the past are crumbling. Today the only intelligent choice is to participate in sex as adult play and an expression of our love. But the roles, the standards and the attitudes crumble slowly, and many have yet to create this choice in their lives. The refusal to make this intelligent choice has caused much to happen before our eyes. And whether what is now happening is good or bad is up to the observer's point of view. Decide for yourself.

Women are successfully competing in the career marketplace. Previously thought of as the "source of life," women now choose to go childless for years, even for life, and to avoid nurturing even their lovers.

There is a decidedly dramatic increase in same-sex romantic and sexual relationships. Men are becoming less macho, women less fragile. Collectively we are becoming more androgynous. Women have progressed from frigidity to multi-orgasmic, while men have plummeted from throbbing studs to impotence. The greatest crime perpetrated by our traditional sexual roles is the illusion that the act of sex is ugly and dangerous. A wondrous form of communication between lovers has been reduced to shameful behavior. Though many of us are learning to rise above such a cruel illusion, it is still evident in our society that lovers have been made to feel unnatural. We are better than this. We are more intelligent than this. We are more honorable than this. As lovers we must choose to be friends. Sex, love and friendship must be joined.

Our traditional seriousness about sex has caused anxiety and disease. And the seriousness that now surrounds sex must, for the sake of alive relationships, transform toward thoughtfulness and compassion for each other. Sex must become safe, fun, friendly, playful, normal and relatively unimportant. Our current obsession with sexual control must become obsolete and ridiculous in much the same way we gave up the primitive fighting over fire. Sexual promiscuity, control and jealousy must become something that belongs to a lower intelligence. "Serious" sex must be recognized as ignorant sex.

More and more people are choosing to enjoy sex with those whom they can honestly call friends, people they know and trust, people with whom they can engage in a way that is playful, satisfying, experimental and safe. When sex is in the news, it is usually linked to disease, crime or failure. But what of another view, that wherever there is beauty and life, there is sex? In this light, it is healthy and communicative. And it is natural for lovers to want to communicate on a deeper level called sex. At this deeper level sex is far more than just a release. At orgasm, your whole body vibrates like electricity.

D.H. Lawrence was taken to court for saying, "There is only one kind of energy, that of our sexuality." Orgasm at this level removes us totally from physical awareness of our partner, and our selves, because at this point transformation occurs. Through orgasm we go to this level of energy. You can only go to this higher frequency if you let go of control and you can only let go with someone you trust. Through trust, boundaries disappear; you no longer consider limitations. It is through this experience that you can, with a friend you can trust, melt and become one. Be attentive and don't miss this experience. You can only have this experience when your partner is both lover and friend. When your partner is only lover or only friend, then only release, ejaculation and relief are possible, but not orgasm, not melting into existence. Orgasm is meeting yourself through your partner. With orgasm, only celebration can happen.

As the trust and love matures, the experience matures. You are timeless together, beyond time and capable of creating your own time. You feel you are willing and want to give everything you have to each other. You feel you are connected, not just on a physical level, but also on an energy level. You are a child again in your mother's womb, absolutely together and all distance is gone. The fact that you are male and female is irrelevant. You are totally free. Just be friends and be playful. Just be lovers and be passionate. Forget about sex. Relax and allow experience to unfold and celebrate being together.

∞

Quality 12

Freedom and Dignity

Within an alive relationship, freedom is the highest quality we can have. Conscious people insist on freedom for themselves and they insist on it for others. For humanity it is instinctive to be free and to be open to change. People in an alive relationship do not force themselves to do anything. They choose to act out of compassion and service rather than duty or obligation. In an alive relationship you do not experience freedom accompanied by any guilt or rejection, you experience freedom as the joy to create. You allow others their freedom even if it causes you sadness. When you have a relationship with the quality of freedom, know that you will be disappointed and sad every now and then. It is a matter of choosing what you value most: freedom, and the reality that you will be sad and disappointed at times, or deficiency and dependence in your life.

Freedom: The primal context from which all creation occurs, from which everything happens. Being able to choose freely and to determine one's own actions.

Dignity: Being worthy of esteem or honor. Dignity is self-respect motivated by love and excitement.

If you want to be with a person who is sitting home waiting for you – and who is jealous of your every move – then your choice is anger and fear. The other choice is to allow the people in your life to have freedom, which means that they are going to make choices. They are going to become self-determined and this means that occasionally you will be rejected. If you want freedom for yourself you must allow it for others because that is the only true freedom. Anything else becomes control of others and that choice will eventually control you. The truth is that only those who are truly free can become close enough to create an alive relationship. Freedom is a higher quality than love because love that is absent of freedom is absent of dignity. And love without dignity ceases to be love.

When you attempt to control others, overtly or covertly, consciously or unconsciously, you are living an illusion and will eventually become so removed from yourself and them that you will not know if they really love you. They will probably just say whatever you want to hear and do things they think you want them to do and all of that creates illusion. When someone is not in relationship by choice there is no freedom and no love, there is only illusion. Often, unconsciously or consciously, people will use their so-called "freedom" to make fun or put others down. This is not freedom. This is hostility. When hostility is manifested it is resentment that keeps you attached and your rebellion becomes a chain around your neck. Your inability to acknowledge those who have contributed to your life robs you of your freedom and dignity. Freedom and dignity are absolutes. They are either present or not present. This is not quantitative. It is holistic.

Freedom and dignity evolve within you when you lose your need for parental authority and when your need to identify and define yourself disappears. At birth we are not free. At birth we are immediately overly defined. We arrive with the following:

- Gender.
- Ethnicity.
- Religion.
- Name.

The process of death by definition continues when we are required to be more and more like Mummy and Daddy, our brothers and sisters and peers. We do this consciously and willingly at first, but at some point we unconsciously define ourselves at the expense of our individual freedom and dignity. We often unconsciously continue doing this throughout our lives and, as a result, destroying our loved ones by overly defining our selves and our relationships. Human beings want freedom because it protects us from definition and humiliation. It protects us from external control and it creates dignity.

When we overly define each other and ourselves we reject freedom because it makes us accountable to ourselves. This is even more frightening because it forces us back on our own abilities and resources. It confronts us with the reality of our aloneness, limitations and insignificance. When we become conscious about our ambivalent relationship with freedom it suddenly becomes obvious, manageable and frequently fun.

Most of us are not aware of our ambivalent relationship with freedom. This lack of awareness is what costs us our dignity. To move beyond your ambivalent relationship with freedom choose or be willing to be:

- Interdependent.
- Alive.
- Instinctive.
- Spontaneous.
- Risk being alone.
- Afraid.
- Confused.
- Hurt.
- Crazy.
- Risk being changed.

Only then you will experience yourself and your relationships as alive. Change will come in the form of a natural trust in you. This allows you to be free and open to experience and to have spontaneous thought and speech rather than having to cautiously repeat, rationalize, defend, justify and need constant validation.

Knowledge of your ambivalent relationship with freedom will eventually cause you to experience your ultimate power and that is your relatedness and the freedom to have a healthy interdependence with your relationships. As your aliveness increases you will experience and accept that you are related and interdependent. You will also acknowledge the contributions your relationships have made and are making to your life. That is power. That is dignity.

Freedom is within. Freedom is formless. It does not look like anything and yet it looks like everything. The key to freedom and dignity is choice not form. Every one of us can be truly free in our own way. Creating freedom and dignity requires being in present time as much as possible and as often as possible. This is how freedom is born and is one of the most satisfying experiences in life. It is aliveness in relationships. Choose to be present, alive, total and complete and out of this you will find your freedom, dignity, authenticity and individuality. You will then know that freedom is our context for our relationships and our aliveness.

Without freedom love cannot exist. Without freedom you are burdened by obligation, which is a form of slavery absent of dignity. Freedom is the garden where aliveness flowers. When you come from freedom, you come from abundance and therefore choice. When you come from need, you come from scarcity and therefore decision or no choice at all.

When the quality of freedom exists in a loving relationship, domination, often experienced as a socially acceptable form of anger, is impossible. Those who are aware share "their love" and support each other's freedom. They are absent of the need to dominate or to compete psychologically. When love is born out of freedom, two or more distinct individuals are experienced as one. Need and dependency forces you to "fall in love," to create illusions and psychological prisons and to experience bondage. If you are conscious lovers, however, you are free to destroy each other's illusions because you know that without freedom there is no love and no happiness.

Freedom is love and loving life. Until you are free you cannot experience yourself as love. This is not a theory. This is an experience available to you right now. Life itself is freedom. There are no contradictions to this. This is not a philosophy. It's simply the way it is. Please receive this and experience yourself as love. Your highest self is screaming to be free. Make a choice. Choose the ultimate responsibility of freedom.

Be aware that freedom is not license. Freedom is not a disregard for agreed upon rules. It's not indulgence in excess. It's not being absent of ethics and responsibilities. Licentiousness is not a manifestation of freedom, but a reaction to slavery. In fact, freedom is not a reaction. It is a way of being rather than an act or event. Freedom is a process, an attitude and a way of living. Those who live freely have their own style, climate and identity. They do not compromise their views or behavior in order to be accepted. Freedom is about choosing your life, your lover, your religion and your career. It's about choosing your education, your way of living each day and each moment.

Once you have chosen your life you will respect that right for others. For example, should your lover choose to love someone more than you, you will not stop them. You will not interfere. You may be sad and hurt and you may suffer and be angry. But you will know the sadness is yours, not theirs. You will not trespass on their freedom.

Many suffer from the conflicting ethic of wanting someone who is not free. We become suspicious of an available person, an easy or competent lover or a free person. We may find ourselves desiring a married person, an unavailable person, a possessed person all the while wondering, "How could an available person be worthwhile?" In those circumstances what we do not realize is that believing "all the good ones are taken" is actually a negative comment about ourselves. Realize in those circumstances that we have learned to thrive more on competition than love, and we behave accordingly. To love someone who is not free or who is unavailable is not love, it is disease.

Free unrestricted love overwhelms and frightens most of us. When we find it, chances are we will no longer be interested. We crave competition, a new fight, a fresh conquest, a proud victory or at least a tantalizing game. Freedom is simply too easy for most of us. We are on ego trips, not love trips. Simple freedom is often beyond our comprehension. On the other hand, those of us who realize the value of freedom also value a higher form of satisfaction. We experience love and pleasure instead of struggle, conquest or competition. When you live and love freely there is no fight. You flow together and everyone in relationship with you is free to flow and choose freely. When you experience yourself as freedom you will be free of this chapter, free to love you and me.

Even when it is available, many of us unconsciously eliminate freedom from our lives because our experience of freedom is one of fear, doubt, insecurity, isolation, alienation and loneliness. Freedom is the ultimate responsibility. It is useful only to those who are willing to take responsibility for their lives. In the broader contexts of concepts such as freedom of speech and political freedom, most of us readily extend those rights to others. But when the context is narrowed and freedom is suggested for our spouse, our child, our employees and others with whom we relate closely, liberals become conservatives. We want freedom for ourselves, but we hesitate to allow it for our loved ones. This is especially true in the area of sexual freedom. Those areas of our lives in which we want to deprive others of freedom are usually those same areas in which we ourselves feel threatened and insecure.

This sense of responsibility can be expressed in every area of our lives. For example, sexual freedom translates to sexual responsibility. Unfortunately, a negative approach to freedom is classic in most of our romantic relationships. When you have had enough you want out of the relationship so you can be free. Then when you are out of the relationship you feel alone, alienated, insecure or even jealous. What often occurs next is a series of in-and-out searches for successful relationships and freedom. If you are caught in this scenario you are caught in an illusion. Being totally together is an illusion as is being totally alone.

The "illusion of freedom" occurs when freedom is symbolically used to escape from anything. That includes authority, control, our relationships or ethnic heritage, our religious heritage and our parents, basically any aspect of life from which we want to escape. When you use freedom as an escape from someone or something this is also an act against that someone or something. Freedom then becomes a character assassination or a put-down of our mother and father, our ethnicity or religion, our husband or wife.

Realize that these relationships are aspects of you so you are actually putting yourself down. Our need to escape, put-down, make wrong and destroy is what keeps us chained to them. Our need to resist is what causes what we resist to persist. The form may change. It may look different. But we are still trapped and at the effect of what we resist. Rather than saying yes we are saying no. Being in rebellion against our parents is the same as obedience to our parents. It just looks different, and it's not freedom. We are still related, and still connected, only in a negative rather than a positive way. Our need to resist, our inability to acknowledge, robs us of our freedom and, more importantly, of our dignity. Be aware that:

- Dignity is an absolute.
- It is either present or not present.
- It is not quantitative. It is holistic.
- You either experience dignity or you do not.
- Absent of dignity we are less than what we can be.
- And we lose our ability to make choices in life.

The solutions are simple. This game can come to an end rather than contribute to a lifetime pattern with which we must live. Just recognize:

- Exemption or liberation from the control of another power or person must be replaced by choosing freely and, therefore, determining your own actions.
- False esteem or pride that engenders being evasive, repressive, defensive, rationalizing or denying must be replaced with dignity.
- Motivation based on your fear and indifference must become motivation stirred by excitement and love.

Most of us experience freedom as the absence of some external pressure when, in truth, it is usually the presence of declared privilege. Religious freedom is usually religious privilege, in which high members have access to other high members and money that are denied other members and non-members. Capitalism is really economic privilege in which the wealthy and upper class have access to goods and services denied lower classes. Communism is really political privilege in which high officials have access to goods and services denied people lower in the party, or especially to those not in the party. Therapy is medical privilege in which physicians and patients have access to drugs and excuses denied to others. Then there is "Single-ism" or promiscuity privilege, "Married-ism" or self-righteous heterosexual and moral privilege, and "Intellectualism" or snob/judgmental privilege.

Understand that all of our freedom has been systematically destroyed by definition. The definitions continue as we are first required and then become anxious to become more and more like Mummy and Daddy. You are familiar with the terms suicide and homicide. But beware of "semanti-cide," which is murder by language and definition. We are constantly murdering our loved ones by definition. We must realize that total freedom or independence is an illusion. Begin to live your life consistent with the idea that "freedom from" is an illusion. Know that "freedom to" requires courage because real freedom is risking being afraid, alone, confused and inevitably changed. It requires being naturally self-determined, a childlike consciousness mixed with the wisdom of experience. Out of the acceptance of "freedom to" you experience:

- Interdependence by choice occurs.
- You become instinctive and spontaneous.
- Our relationships become alive.
- We speak originally and openly rather than consciously repeating.
- We think openly without justifying and defending.
- We realize that real freedom in a relationship is to have a healthy interdependence.
- We experience our relatedness and power.
- We reach the natural acceptance that we are related, that we are dependent by choice, that we are aware of the contribution people have made and are making to our life.

"Freedom to" is a commitment to love and excitement. When you deny the contributions made to you by others and avoid acknowledging others, you avoid:

- You.
- Your relationships.
- Your heritage.
- Your origin.
- Your awareness.

All of this avoidance results in "independence" and that is today's word for loneliness. True freedom is interdependence and that is the law of the universe. It is choice, not the form in which the choice manifests. Real freedom is within, whether you are married or single, Christian or Jew, young or old, male or female. Freedom has nothing to do with form when you are in that form by choice. Real freedom does not look like anything. Real freedom feels like aliveness, happiness and passion, and is absent of effort and struggle. Freedom has no form. The key to freedom is choice.

∞

Quality 13

The Ability to be Alone Together

Few people are capable of spending time alone. That is why most people are in horrible relationships and why so many are incapable of finding others who will respect their space. I have never been able to tolerate people with a lot of mind chatter. People with "busy brains" are always overflowing with thoughts. Not their own thoughts, but the trash they have accumulated during the day and then leak all over everyone around them. I genuinely appreciate people who are capable of entertaining themselves, people who are occupied by their own lives. There is nothing worse than being totally involved in a project while someone sits in the room waiting to interrupt you with their manifestations of boredom.

Life is about transformation. It is about changing in relationship. It is about moving from one definition to another, from stranger to friend, to lover, to old friend, etc. The ability to be away from somebody or close to somebody, whether you are in the same room or not, is the ability to be alone or "all-one." Often my experience of the holding-on clinging kind of love is really someone being threatened by someone else's freedom and by someone else's will to be his or her own self.

Alone: Complete, whole, all-one.

Most of us do not fully understand the positive and fulfilling experience of being alone, that act of being all-one, of being complete. This feeling of aloneness has nothing to do with loneliness, which is an absence of self. The ability of being alone is:

- To be totally present.
- To be complete unto yourself.
- To be okay about yourself.
- And to be comfortable in your body, mind, spirit and environment.

The ability to be alone allows us to be capable of being together with someone else. No matter how gregarious or charming or loving we think we are, we must have an accepting relationship with ourselves before we are capable of successfully relating to anyone else. This is a pre-requisite for an alive relationship. The majority of us cannot stand being alone because, absent of external stimuli, our unconscious mind cycles disturbing unresolved images. When we are alone our mind starts re-creating memories of the past and fears of the future, causing upsets and anxiety.

In our society it is nearly impossible to spend quality time with our selves. Most of us have traveled swiftly from the womb to our mother's arms, to school, to work, to marriage, to the military, to university and on to the world of work and have never really been alone. It seems reasonable that it be required, or at least encouraged, to take some time out of high school or college, strap on a backpack and learn to survive on our own. We are culturally inexperienced at being on our own so our relationships are born out of the fear of being alone. We often go into relationships not by choice, but out of fear and need.

When we go into a relationship out of the fear of being alone the relationship is false and usually short-lived. Unless we transform out of the fear, we will eventually be disappointed as will our partner. When fear of being alone is the root of our primary relationships, love becomes the inability to be alone and becomes our insecurity. Our partner then provides an escape from ourselves and enables us to avoid dealing with ourselves. It is our partner that we will eventually despise for this enabling just as we despise anything or anyone upon whom we become dependent: alcohol, drugs, a job or another human being. A relationship created out of the inability to be alone inevitably turns love into dependence, or worse, desperation. When aloneness becomes loneliness, love becomes hate. We do not consciously know what is wrong and we do not even remember the sequence of how it all happened.

The solution is to first experience being alone joyously and then choose to have a relationship. That choice is the outcome of truly valuing the people in our life. We can only be with people joyfully when we do not depend upon them for happiness. A good example of this is the myth of "unhappy only children" who are without playmates and no one to entertain them. What is generally true is that "only children" actually do better in life primarily because they are capable of entertaining themselves; they are self-determined; they are their own source of joy; they are willing to share their happiness with others; they do not experience relationship as a burden but rather as a privilege; they are more sensitive to the opportunity to be compassionate and loving.

We must first have the courage to experience loneliness and, while witnessing it, allow it to transform into oneness. We must also have the courage to be alone in order to experience not needing others for our happiness. When we have had the conscious experience of being alone joyously, only then can we enter into an alive relationship that flows at the level of the power of choice. To choose a relationship we love, we must first enjoy being alone. The power of aloneness (all-oneness) then can be shared together. Togetherness is delusion and loneliness is illusion. Both are transcended with the courage to be our selves and to share our self with another. We come into this life alone and we will go out alone. When we take a moment to contemplate this we value the contributions our relationships make in our lives.

The illusion of togetherness comes out of our fear of being alone because simply being alone, absent of stimulus, we are most likely to create all of our thoughts as realities. Some of these we detest and do not want to face. At first, being alone is like watching a horror movie or, at best, a depressing true-life drama. We get caught up in the negative experiences. These are most often re-experienced because the severity of intense negative emotions is easier to play on our mental screen. Relationships are often just a distraction from our aloneness, a kind of camouflage so that we can't truly see ourselves. We play the field searching for the right person eventually accepting the not-so-right mate.

When we are honest, and look deeply, we have been avoiding ourselves our entire lives. We distract ourselves in different ways. We fall in love with men, women, money, power, cars, religion and the list goes on. With courage and clarity all can be reduced to one single motive, the fear of being alone. Since childhood, we have willingly given away our power to whomever or whatever distracted us from ourselves. We grow up learning what other people thought, and most of them thought that alone is synonymous with lonely and that being alone means being miserable. The illusion continues as we search for the next avoidance of self in which to drown ourselves: television, sports, sex, drugs, alcohol, work, etc. Any diversion will do. With our convenient crutches we forget that we are lonely and go on, occasionally changing the activity or the excuse. The solution is to experience our authenticity. The cure for what seems to be a never-ending cycle is to:

- Be yourself.
- Just be you.
- Have no pretense.
- Have no excuses.

Transforming loneliness to aloneness is painful for most of us because our aloneness forces us to face ourselves. Suddenly we are able to see our emptiness and become frightened. At this point one of two things occurs. We begin to literally die a slow unconscious death or we choose to become aware. When we choose the latter, we realize that awareness of loneliness creates togetherness and that loneliness creates more loneliness. With awareness loneliness transforms into aloneness. The experience of being alone is finally experienced as completion and as power, the power to be alone together. Awareness, which is achieved through aloneness, is the opportunity to be extraordinary. It is the opportunity to transform, to experience the truth and become powerful.

Aloneness cannot be avoided. It must be accepted. The path is to go into it and become it. Awareness and alive relationships cannot be acquired unless we encounter our aloneness. Aloneness does not create new information. It creates transformation. Aloneness does not allow us the comfort of the lie of togetherness, the luxury of distraction or the convenience of living in illusion. We live in a society filled with illusions and suddenly finding yourself alone hurts and can be depressing. Every time we examine our illusions we become depressed. When we lose a lover our depression is usually caused not by what we had, but what we could have had together and the things we planned to do, which never materialized.

With awareness we experience aloneness as complete, we can examine our illusions and allow them to disappear. This emptiness is the absence of illusion and is your home, your source and your origin. It is peaceful. In time we enjoy it and demand our time alone. We come to know this aloneness as the source of our creativity. With ironic energy we recall our ignorant past self that diligently worked at avoiding itself. Once we have arrived at the awareness of aloneness we may see our mind playing tricks. Illusions return in one form or another whenever we forget our power. But at this stage little effort is needed to drop the illusions. All that is required is the realignment with our power.

Illusions are like bad habits. If we forget they tend to reappear. My father was an amateur boxer and we often had boxers like Grazziano or Marciano in the house. One of the jokes they told illustrates the concept of fighting illusions: An aging boxer phoned his old manager, "Sammy! I wanna fight Killer Olson." – "No," replied the manager. "Your fighting days are done. How many times do I have to tell you?" – "But, please Sammy. I know I can beat him. Please, Sammy, just one more fight." – "No," said Sammy. "There is no need to fight. Enjoy your life. Quit while you're still walking." – "But Sammy," pleaded the old fighter, "Why can't I fight the Killer?" – With contempt and compassion the manager replied, "You can't you fight Killer Olson because you are Killer Olson!"

The fights are our illusions of togetherness. We are the boxer. Killer is who we were before and our awareness is the manager who goes on yelling. Loneliness and togetherness are both illusions and they keep us going back for more: just one more relationship, just one more marriage, just one more divorce or just one more romance. We must get past the illusions of loneliness and togetherness, divorce and marriage. They are polarities, opposites of the same illusion. When we live our life in fear of being alone we die terrified. The fear of death is an outcome of our indulgence in the illusion of togetherness. What we actually fear about death is not the unknown. What we truly fear is the separation from our illusions.

Most of us have never been alone and therefore do not know who we are without a relationship. Our relationships act as mirrors that help us identify, define and label ourselves. Without mirrors there is a great abyss, a huge void. When we go into this void we become afraid. In our efforts to minimize that fear we become imitators. We become part of a crowd. We join clubs, churches and groups. We go into relationships. We want to be a part of something or someone in order to avoid our aloneness. Because most of us have never spent any time alone, we tend not to differentiate between loneliness and aloneness. Loneliness is the absence of another. Aloneness is the presence of one-self. When you understand the difference you know your power and have discovered your source. To be capable of love we must be capable of being alone. A lonely person is unable to love. With our ability to be alone we know that:

- We can have many people around us and not need them.
- We are capable of loving everyone and express that love with whomever we choose.
- We are capable of being ourselves.
- We are capable of being with others and allow them to be.
- We are capable and willing to be intimate with others.
- We are willing to be in our relationships.
- We are at ease with others when we are at ease with ourselves.
- We are happy with ourselves and do not need anyone else for our happiness.
- We give and are willing to share our joy.

The prerequisite and the initial and critical lesson of an alive relationship is the ability to be alone. So we must:

- Go through our loneliness.
- Go through the feelings of anger, sadness and pain.
- Watch our mind as it creates frightening thoughts.
- Experience the perception of monotony and boredom.
- Interpret the illusions and the fantasies.

Being alone is just a simple form of sensory deprivation. At first the brain does not appreciate being by itself. Absent of outside stimulation our awareness goes inside and when it has run out of inside information it will begin to create fantasies. This is one of the reasons why we dream. We dream when our physical world disappears. When we are alone our brain supplies the stimulus. In time we learn to control the form of stimulus or turn it off altogether. One of the greatest miracles and pleasures of life is to be alone with ourselves, absent of illusion and fantasy, and allow others to be the way they are. Only then can we truly be with someone else and experience an alive relationship.

When we have experienced all the stages of being alone, we begin to feel at home in our body and mind. What felt like loneliness at first becomes the experience of our being and we feel related to everyone and everything. We are happy for no reason at all. This does not mean that others cannot bring us happiness, for they obviously do. But always remember when our happiness is dependent on others our unhappiness will also be caused by others. Reliance on others means that our happiness will always be uncertain.

To be alone together is to be absolutely free. Our happiness will be unthreatened by either the absence or the presence of another person. When we are experiencing this absolute state of being all-one not even death frightens us because we know death only separates us from others, but not ourselves. For most of us the concept of death is eternal loneliness. It lurks in the shadows with the death of a loved one, a parent, relationship, friendship or career. Death can be accepted as an expected transformation once we have experienced the ultimate power of being alone (all-one) together. The price is cheap. The price is to experience loneliness first. Go through it.

Then we experience a relationship with ourselves that makes it possible to be alone together with whomever we choose. The ability to be alone together is the willingness and capability to have a private experience within our relationships. Remember, only you can do it and you can't do it alone.

∞

Quality 14

Creativity

When the quality of creativity exists our relationships transform. Problems change into opportunities rather than situations that we fear or fail. With creativity there is a willingness to correct and we have a high tolerance for mistakes. People in alive relationships are willing to create and risk bringing something new into being, even when that requires "letting go" or destroying what they have.

Creativity: To make a distinction and cause what is already there. Creativity is clarity on what is. What this means in terms of our relationships is:

- To be inventive.
- The willingness to let go of what you have and create anew.

As children we were conditioned to avoid creating. We were told such things as: "Oh, you just made that up." or "You're just saying that." or "Be realistic." or "Be reasonable." We learned to avoid creative action by taking noncreative action. Eventually most of us stopped taking any responsibility for our ability to create.

Creativity requires focused, meaningful work prior to breakthrough or actualization. This usually never happens on the first attempt since creativity is often contrary to our conditioning and comfort. When we risk going beyond the limits of conditioning, and allow things to unfold creatively, problems and difficulties cease to exist. Each effort becomes the opportunity to enjoy, to experience satisfaction and to have the chance to participate.

Creativity is a quality. It is not a single act, but rather an attitude that you bring to the relationship. Our intelligence, understanding and experience of any activity is directly proportional to the level of creativity brought to the activity. This intelligence creates and brings into the world something new. Creativity makes the world richer and more beautiful. It creates new truths. Creative problem solving in alive relationships becomes a by-product of our:

- Boldness.
- Courage.
- Freedom.
- Spontaneity.
- And integrity.

The outcome is higher unity and wholeness. In alive relationships creativity is a joyous and healthy interaction. It is sometimes absent of any great talent, but it always comes in the form of a unique contribution to one's self and others. Be aware that healthy and alive creativity is not essentially connected to special talent.

Although those in alive relationships do not necessarily exhibit sparks of great talent or genius, they are, or have the capability to be, creative in special ways.

Creative people include business people, homemakers and students. A skilled musician playing someone else's composition may play flawlessly, but a gardener, dressmaker or mechanic may be more creative. Special talent is one thing, but creativity is a by-product of our aliveness, spontaneity, courage, freedom and integrity. It is everything we do and an outcome of who we are, rather than what we have studied. Creative people are:

- Spontaneous.
- Natural, less controlled and uninhibited.
- Without fear of ridicule, encourage feedback and correction from sources they respect.
- Free of stereotype.
- Open to experience.
- Follow no prescribed pattern.
- Simultaneously playful and responsible.
- Less conditioned.
- Not obsessed with what people are saying about them.
- Less afraid of themselves and trust their instincts.

Creative people trust themselves and their own experiences of life. They have confidence in their processes, perceptions and uniqueness and move more toward being themselves rather than another's concept of who they are. They move toward their own thoughts, more toward themselves. Creation is to "screw it up." Every artist knows the value of certain mistakes:

- Creativity is the art of inventiveness.
- Creativity is synonymous with being alive.

When we are creative we radiate aliveness. We love problems and thrive on solutions, as these are opportunities for inventiveness. Alive relationships are not necessarily artistic or intellectual, but they are inspiring and inventive. When we are in alive relationships we:

- Flow.
- Have fewer blocks.
- Don't engage in a lot of self-criticism.
- Are childlike rather than childish.

- Are an adult who has reclaimed our power.
- Are open to experience.
- Are expressive, perceptive and innocent.
- Relatively unafraid of the unknown.
- We drop our childhood conditioning to "do things the right way" and know the key to creativity is to be willing to "do things the wrong way."

Creative people are not afraid to express their thoughts and emotions. They are willing to expose their crazy and silly sides. Their inhibitions and plans don't get in their way. They allow themselves and their relationships to be emotional, therefore, are more whole and integrated than average and create more of them selves to be available. Each of us is born with creativity, but to remain creative we must risk. We must refuse to get stuck in the memories of education, religion and "the way things are." Creativity has nothing to do with the form it takes. To creative people washing windows is creative and they experience less frustration and drudgery, bringing a semblance of joy to their chores. To creative people work and play are the same and an alive relationship is one in which elements of life are being created that have not existed before.

∞

Quality 15

Healing

One of the unique advantages of alive relationships is that you consciously heal each other. Part of the reason is that you experience your partner's healing personally, being available for them so they can heal themselves through you. If you are unaware of this you are probably unhappy and will continue to be unhappy. To heal a physical wound the wound must be open. Bandages have holes to vent the wound. To heal an emotional wound you must also be open, available and vulnerable. Each time you are hurt you have to be courageous and open up. This is not easy because the potential for being hurt again continues to exist. Yet this is the only way to heal. The alternative is to shut down, create disease and experience the death of relationship.

Healing: To restore a greater wisdom to our physical, emotional, mental and spiritual bodies. This requires affinity and courage.

Affinity: The occupation of the same idea or thoughts resulting in the attraction of a greater wisdom.

Courage: The willingness to act when failure is possible.

Vulnerability is essential to the healing process. Most people, especially men, believe that being vulnerable is not only dangerous, but is also weak. The truth is that to be vulnerable requires you to be extremely healthy and confident. You have to really love yourself to be vulnerable and willing to accept the risk. One of the rewards of alive relationships is the possibility of healing incomplete emotional and psychological traumas, both in yourself and in your partners, which occurs when compassion is present. Compassion is being conscious of the contribution someone is making to your life.

If you do not expect this healing process in significant relationships it is time to evaluate whether you are willing to relate. When you allow healing to occur, the healing process takes effect and your partner will become healed in the relationship with you, not in one conjured from the past. We often create our partners to be what we think they are going to be. Then when they become it we get angry and say, "I knew you would eventually act like this." Or we enter a new relationship and fear it is going to be like the last one. We invariably create the same relationship because we become what we fear and we do the same things that we did in the last relationship until, one day, we wake up and realize we've again married our mother or father.

To heal basic actions need to be taken. Here are some of the basic actions, which result in healing the self and our relationships:

• We must heal our relationship to God, existence or whatever we choose to call the consciousness humanity has attempted for millennium to explain. None of our relationships will be experienced in a joyous and ecstatic way until we are clear about our concept of God. Otherwise we go through life either blaming God or believing God will punish us or that God is out to get us. What is amazing is the number of people who see God through anxious eyes. Many operate unconsciously as if God is a sadist. There are those who are always asking God for something as if God is their personal servant. Others live out a type of paranoia believing God is personally watching them and is the ultimate authority. God has always been a difficult concept to understand. Some chase God and become life long seekers while others run from God and join the agnostics and the atheists.

- The simple truth: God is existence. God just is. God is the source of everything and therefore our source. Once this simplicity is accepted we realize the futility of attempting to run away from our source. God is the source from which everything and everyone comes and when we do not have a good relationship with our source how can we have a good relationship with people? In some languages the origin of the word "God" means "good" and the words remain synonymous. Perhaps that's been the error, to separate the two, to separate God and good. How can we love people and not love God? How can we love the creation and not love the creator? We are part of the source. We are inseparable. Those who attempt to separate themselves from God are like waves attempting to exist without an ocean. God is existence. God is aliveness expressed in our thoughts and relationships. God is simply more of us, our source.

- Healing occurs when you live our life consistent with the understanding that thought is creative. This happens through healing and forgiving our relationships. As thinkers we are creative with our thoughts and create the thoughts that produce our relationships. Negative and positive thoughts produce corresponding relationships. Whatever we think about we manifest. We must recognize and eventually clear our old thoughts, such as: "women are my mother" and "men are my father." These old basic thoughts produce more thoughts, such as: "women are maternal, over-protective, trying to trap, suffocate or destroy me." What we forget is we are the thinker, both the garden and the gardener, who created maternal, controlling, over-bearing women, or paternal, controlling, overbearing men. As the thinker we are able to create supportive women or men who truly want us to be free to be ourselves and to be healthy and powerful. To create our relationships anew we must use repetitive, positive thoughts charged with emotion. These will eventually replace old outdated modes of thinking and eventually erase them.

• When we do not heal and forgive our relationships every unresolved relationship from the past drains the aliveness from our present relationships. Forgiving old relationships results in the immediate experience of aliveness in present relationships. It is vital that we clear up anything unresolved with our parents. We must transcend any unwillingness and forgive our parents. As soon as we forgive our parents a recognizable shift will occur. The shift may bring up historic pain, which can be healed in present time and with our present partner. Or we will no longer be willing to be treated in certain ways, reflective of our past, and find a new partner. Our present relationships are often unconsciously attempting to heal us and unknowingly act out negative roles similar to those of past relationships. We can recognize this opportunity and become aware of what is happening and to heal ourselves.

• We must heal, forgive and love ourselves. It has taken years to create our relationships. We have learned that people treat us basically the way we treat ourselves and the faster we forgive and love ourselves the faster we create the opportunity for others to heal us. When we dislike or even hate ourselves we are a victim and victims are incurable skeptics unwilling to be healed or loved. What's true is that no one knows enough to be skeptical. Human beings don't have enough understanding, of our selves or our species, our minds or our capabilities, to be skeptical. We're too ignorant. To heal yourself, you must:

- Acknowledge yourself.
- Approve of your actions.
- Admire your abilities.
- Give yourself pleasure.
- Drop your guilt.
- Love your body.
- Give yourself what you want.

- Allow others to heal and love you.
- Appreciate your uniqueness.
- Give up poverty.
- Reward yourself.
- Trust and nourish yourself.
- Enjoy affection and sex.
- Reverse negative thinking.
- Give up covert anger and suppressed negativity.

Our "dis-ease" is created by suppressed anger and negative thought. One of the reasons our loving relationships tend to heal us best is that love brings up everything unlike love itself. Love brings up anger, sadness, fear, pain, jealousy, uncontrollable upset and other negative experiences. This is a healing process. It is our current experience of love re-stimulating all our historic negative experience with love. This re-stimulation process makes the historic, forgotten experiences conscious and allows us to heal ourselves. Ultimately, if we allow it, love always heals. What's true is that we are never upset for the reason we think. What is happening in present time is usually old anger and resentment we have yet to release.

Once we have experienced the rewards of forgiving we know that blame has no value. To discover your patterns of repeating notice when you:

- Give up guilt. Know that guilt always attracts relationships that fit our patterns. An example is a woman who believes in her heart that "men leave me." The result is that this woman attracts men who have a pattern of leaving. Guilt has been around for so long that most of us consider it to be a feeling. But guilt is a strategy, a thought and a method for getting others to do things they don't want to do out of "duty" or "obligation" or "higher religious calling." The "guilty" are easy to identify: they think pleasure is bad; that fun is a waste of time; they are always understanding and reasonable; usually non-expressive and reach their pleasure tolerance quickly.

• Get clarity on sex and jealousy. Sex is a miraculous creative behavior that allows us to transcend our form. Realize that we deserve sexual pleasure because sex is fun and passion is a form of adult play. Eliminate all of your archaic sexual beliefs, which do not support your experience of sex as pleasurable. The cure for jealousy is self-esteem. When someone leaves you experience this as their loss, not yours. Jealousy is an outcome of the illusion that you own or have title to someone else's body and mind. Self-esteem is the power and the consciousness to acknowledge, correct, improve and create a better relationship than the last without the pain of jealousy. Be aware of unconsciously creating your partners to be like your father or mother. The more our mate becomes like a parent the less you are able to enjoy sex with each other.

• Keep your relationships in present time as much as possible.

We cannot clear up anything we cannot communicate. Don't pretend to get over an upset. Work through it. Never suppress your feelings or you will eventually overflow and begin to dump on everyone. Choose to consciously forgive and begin each day as a new relationship. Clear out your psychic garbage. One of the basic failures of modern psychology is that it often requires us to read our garbage before we throw it away. Just let it go. Be clear that our capacity to love and to heal is directly proportional to the quality of our communication.

∞

Quality 16

Forgiveness as a State of Consciousness

We perceive forgiveness as a single act that we do once, or sometimes more than once, for another person. We often consider forgiveness as a compromise, an act that can cause us to lose our dignity. Genuine forgiveness, however, is not a single act. It is not even a decision that we make. We may mouth the words, but we don't really decide whether to forgive or not to forgive. Forgiveness in its true state is a process. It is a state of being, a high state of consciousness that we become and from which we operate. It is being empty, open and absent of judgment. It is giving up the need and the power to control someone or to get even. We achieve this state after enormous work when we finally become ourselves.

Forgive: The continuous process of giving up resentment and the desire to punish; to stop being angry; to let go of power and control over others.

When we are not operating from forgiveness, we are not the person we are capable of being. When we move past our tendencies toward judgment and resentment we are able to achieve a genuinely alive experience of our relationships. The initial discomfort we experience in clearing our brain of resentment becomes worthwhile. It allows us to function at a new level where we experience the ability to talk to anyone. With this new clarity we are able to be with anyone without form, mannerisms or judgmental behavior determining our self-confidence or aliveness.

When we are operating from forgiveness it does not matter if people are black or white, male or female, young or old, Arab or Jew, gay or straight. We are beyond that at will and by choice.

Forgiving your parents is the most important process of forgiveness to complete. Becoming consciously forgiving toward your parents frees you to become you. It does not matter if they are alive or dead. In fact, if your parents are dead, the process is easier. They are no longer capable of hurting you and therefore completion should be easier. But regardless of their aliveness or proximity, forgiving your parents is essential to your aliveness. Forgiveness creates the immediate experience of happiness, joy and relief.

Forgiveness is a selfish act and the person you are forgiving does not even have to know that you have forgiven them. The release happens anyway. The joy is inevitable and it is yours. It will help if you remember:

- The way we perceive people is the way they are.
- We create things the way we think about them.
- The opportunity to change how we think about someone, including ourselves, is always present.
- Forgiving allows us to have a sense of humor.

We regain a sense of humor about ourselves as well as about the human condition. We understand that life is just a series of events and circumstances that we created and in which we can find far-reaching value. We also realize that our parents are one of those circumstances. We did not fill out any forms for them nor did they fill out any forms for us. We just got each other. To remain angry over circumstance is to remain ignorant and an avoidance of the capable, loving you. To be alive is to find the value in our parental relationships and all the others that followed. Always be aware that forgiveness is a process and not an act. Remaining in a state of forgiveness is an important key to your aliveness.

∞

Quality 17

Assertiveness

The results you create in life are directly proportional to the degree to which you are skillfully assertive. Most of us suffer from a lifetime of inhibitive conditioning that causes us to think that we don't have the right to be assertive. We are often corrected for being assertive so whenever this essential skill is necessary we become anxious and fearful.

Assertiveness: The skill of expressing, affirming and stating positively your creativity while also contributing to your alive relationships.

The greatest myth about assertiveness is that you either have it or you don't. Assertiveness is not a birthright or a character trait. It is a skill that can be chosen and learned. When assertiveness is present in an alive relationship the individuals act as a unified team. They state their position and courageously affirm themselves. They are spontaneously honest, expressing their feelings and keeping the relationship alive in present time. They insist on their personal rights, and those of others, and create dignity in the process. They think of all the results in life as being within "their reality" when they are willing to create them.

There are really only three ways to be in a relationship and that is to be:

- Aggressive.
- Assertive.
- Or non-assertive.

Aggressive behavior is really outward-directed anger. Non-assertive behavior is inner-directed anger or fear. Both create unconscious results and damage all of our relationships. Assertive behavior creates the results you choose and contributes to the self-esteem and wellbeing of each of your relationships. Assertiveness is not aggressiveness. It means being aware of the rights of all involved. When this has been understood and courageously pursued what occurs in our relationships is:

- Open intimacy.
- Self-expression.
- Effective communication.
- Self-esteem.
- And creativity.

New values emerge in alive relationships. Today there is more honesty and self-expression at home and at school, in our work and personal lives. In intimate relationships women are taking the initiative. Men are being freed of the expectant first-move responsibility and are learning how to receive rather than merely perform. Most importantly, both males and females now have the right and conviction to say "yes" or "no" honorably. Both sexes have begun to move towards more balanced roles. Both can be the nurturer and provider. To achieve and maintain these new roles, assertiveness, especially with a loved one, is essential. The basic aspects of assertiveness are:

- Expressing the true you.
- Honesty.
- Directness or firmness.
- Respect for the rights of others.
- Alignment with your environment.
- Social responsibility.
- Most importantly, enhancement of yourself and others.

Many people become anxious and fearful even when assertiveness is appropriate because we have been conditioned that being assertive is pushy and offensive or we confuse it for aggression. Most of us are blocked about the value of being assertive because:

1. We do not believe we have the right to be assertive, an outcome of our conditioning to withhold and be non-assertive. Most of us are emerging from a lifetime of unconscious voices insisting:

- "Be still."
- "Don't you dare talk to your mother/father that way."
- "Children should be seen and not heard."
- "Never let me hear you say that again."
- "Stop crying or I'll give you something to cry about."
- "Shut up when I'm talking to you."

2. We are anxious and fearful about being assertive. As children, we were put down and made to feel fearful about school or family. As adults, we were fearful of most public situations. When we were assertive:

- People in the room became still and quiet.
- All attention was directed toward us.
- Lovers and friends left us.
- We experienced discomfort.
- We were singled out as disruptive.
- We were accused of being a bad person.

3. We believe we lack the inborn talent needed to be assertive. Believing it is inherent in certain personalities so we go through life not developing the skill in our relationships. When you are unable to be assertive you go through life:

- Withholding until you explode with anger.
- Inhibited.
- Giving into the wishes of others.
- Holding your desires inward.
- Destroying others to get your way.
- Possessing low self-esteem and unable to create.

4. Finally, we were taught that being reasonable was a good thing and that to be patient is the golden rule. What's true is that being reasonable is as close to death as you can get while still breathing. Assertive action always creates alive relationships because:

- We are acting in our own best interests.
- We state our position and affirm ourselves absent of fear or anxiety.
- We express honest feelings, moving into present time, creating happiness and spontaneity.
- We exercise our personal rights without denying the rights of others, creating personal power and dignity for everyone.
- We systematically acquire self-esteem, causing aliveness.

Assertiveness means to state positively, to claim, declare and affirm. Yet most people experience it as anger and aggression. Genuine assertiveness has nothing to do with maligning others or denying their rights and feelings. It is true that assertiveness is often discouraged because it is confused with aggression. This attitude causes us to experience a lower level of satisfaction in all areas of our lives. Our families continue withholding. Because their ability to be openly assertive is suppressed children eventually become rebellious and destructive. As many parents learn, unconscious accidents soon follow.

In our educational system students are rarely encouraged to speak up, to disagree or to express original thought, especially if their thinking is superior to that of their teacher or fellow students. Educators openly admit that a child's natural spontaneity for learning is conditioned out of them by the fourth or fifth grade. We are sedating and discouraging the intelligence of our children.

In our business enterprises individuals are discouraged from being assertive, from rocking the boat, or they may risk losing raises and promotions. The pressure is on to conform to the system. At the mall youth appear mesmerized by superficial chatter, mindless eating and populist consumption. Organized religions praise meekness and preach surrender to a higher power, which unfortunately translates into surrender, not to God, but the middleman. Examples of the greatest rebels, such as Buddha, Christ and Mohammed, reflect the truest nature of assertiveness. Rebelliousness today is outside the bounds of organized religion. Instead, to be religious is to be humble so to be accepted by religious authority is to accept self-sacrifice and self-denial.

And if we want a loving and romantic relationship, assertiveness, while necessary, also leads to the risk of your partner leaving. That thought scares a lot of people out of whatever assertiveness they had resulting in exactly what they don't want to happen, a dead relationship. The result of all this conditioning against assertiveness has caused us to limit:

- Open intimacy.
- Self-expression.
- Honest communications.
- Self-esteem.
- The power to create.

Unfortunately, most of society still discourages assertiveness because we still have the social ideal of the passive, sweet, submissive, accepting, nurturing, sympathetic woman and the strong, active, decisive, cool, dominant, rational man. Since the 1970s, society has begun to value assertive women. A new ideal of forthrightness and honesty has emerged. This ideal at first appears to be aggressive only because we have not yet dropped all of the old destructive ethics. We are gradually replacing them with new ethics that are contributing to our aliveness and therefore our future.

Men are letting go of the macho protector and sole provider mold. They are choosing to be genuine and vulnerable. In increasing numbers, men are insisting on self-esteem and respect rather than the fear of not having them. As they mature into this new awareness they are beginning to feel that achievements acquired through aggression mean little and provide only brief satisfaction. Men are discovering the value of:

- Personal intimacy.
- Trusted friendships.
- Family closeness, openness and honesty are the lasting and important achievements.

To be assertive is to be willing to make choices. Assertiveness is the personal power and high level of esteem that enables you to act in your best interest and to make your own choices about your career, your relationships, your lifestyle and your time. You can take the initiative to:

- Start conversations.
- Organize activities.
- Participate socially.
- Ask for the support of others.
- Trust yourself.

You can choose to stand up for yourself by:

- Saying no.
- Setting limits on time.
- Setting limits on energy.
- Responding to correction.
- Responding to put-downs.
- Responding to anger.
- Expressing your self.

We can choose to express honest feelings by:

- Disagreeing and agreeing.
- Showing anger responsibly.
- Showing affection.
- Showing friendship.
- Being spontaneous.

You must also be competent as:

- A consumer/seller.
- An employee/employer.
- A parent/child.
- A citizen.
- A lover/spouse.

And most importantly, respecting the rights of others involves accomplishing all of the above without unnecessary criticism, irresponsible gossip, intimidation, negative manipulation or controlling others without their consent. Assertiveness is positive self-affirmation, which contributes to everyone in your life. It also allows you to value that contribution.

There are consequences for the non-assertive, the aggressive and the assertive relationship. When we are in a non-assertive relationship we are self-denying, inhibited, easily hurt, anxious and living our life consistent with others choices. We are not creating our aliveness. When you are in a relationship with a non-assertive person you are guilty, angry, not valuing your relationships and creating chosen results often at the expense and detriment of your non-assertive partner. When we are in an aggressive relationship we are self-enhancing at the expense of our partner, negatively expressive, constantly choosing for others and hurting our partner.

When we are in a relationship with an aggressive person we are self-denying, hurt, angry, defensive, humiliated and not creating aliveness. When we are an assertive person we are self-enhancing, expressive, feeling good and making our own choices. In a relationship with an assertive person we experience equality. The assertive person neither hurts self nor partner intentionally and both people in the relationship are likely to be successful and happy. This is simple, but like any skill it requires practice.

∞

Quality 18

The Joy of Laughter, Humor and Playfulness

Together, the traits of laughter, humor and playfulness represent a joyous state in which we are willing to be foolish and playful in relationships and get out of our brain or beyond what current technology considers our brain. In this state we have a non-serious sincerity, aliveness and a willingness to be anything. In this state we joyously relinquish our image of a rational adult to become more childlike. But do not confuse childlike with childish. In our society most believe that seriousness is somehow synonymous with honesty, effectiveness and sincerity. This is false.

Laughter: An ecstatic state of consciousness, which occurs beyond thought.

Humor: A state of awareness that experiences the condition of humanity and one's self with ironic pleasure.

Playfulness: A conscious and childlike state.

I don't recall a time in my life when seriousness was of value. I have sat and watched and evaluated for years, but I am convinced that seriousness has no value in and of itself. When viewed consciously, seriousness is a disease-oriented and destructive behavior. When people ask me to "listen seriously" to what they are saying, I politely reply, "No thanks. I will listen and be sincere about what you are saying, but I will not be serious."

Employers tend to demand this of their employees as if it reflects competence and productivity; in fact, seriousness generally produces stagnation and lethargy, which ultimately results in less productivity. We've known for years that, when enjoying themselves, people learn faster, have greater retention and are more productive and creative. A sense of humor is a mental state in which you can be sincere with people without being heavy. It is smiling at the possibility that there may be no divine purpose for you being alive other than to have a good time.

Recognizing this also allows us to know that God, rather than being sadistic, wants you to enjoy your life. Maybe you will conclude you were sent in from Central Casting like the rest of us! Recognizing our humorous nature has much to do with not taking our selves too seriously. The people who make it in life are the ones who laugh. Laughter is beyond the brain. It heals and is essential to our survival and the survival of our alive relationships. When you develop your sense of humor your relationships become more playful, spontaneously alive and you are able to have fun and re-create together.

Do you really want to be in a relationship with someone who is serious all of the time? It certainly happens. I've seen lovers sit in restaurants and talk about their relationship rather than enjoy their relationship. Stop talking and go live your relationship. Go dancing. Go to a movie. Work together. Make love. Create together. Or just simply be with each other. Do something. Anything. Participate and share rather than observe and blame.

All those serious discussions will destroy your aliveness and everyone in relationship with you. Who brings this seriousness out in you? That would be someone who has an investment in death. That would be someone with whom you should spend less time. Seriousness and anger, as I've stated before, are the roots of "dis-ease." Conversely, laughter is the healer. Beware of seriousness. Be aware and laugh.

Laughter and the absence of thought occur simultaneously. They are inseparable spiritual qualities beyond our brain. They are expressions of life itself. They are our aliveness, our inborn nature. They are metaphysical qualities. Total laughter is rare. It occurs when every cell of our body vibrates and it ends in a deep relaxation. Who brings this out in you? Who creates this within you? This is someone with whom you are sharing love. This total deep laughter is the active form of love. This is someone with whom it's wise to spend more time.

We cannot study or rehearse true laughter. It is beyond rehearsal. It is natural, spontaneous and everyone can do it. No preparation is possible. Playfulness and laughter do not rely on our ego. In their fullest sense, it is as if we are having an out-of-body experience, as if joy has possessed us. What's true is that when we laugh we become a passageway, a vehicle for the expression of our aliveness.

Few places remain in our society where the expression of total laughter is allowed. If you look around it appears as if laughter was deemed contrary to life. Some people become upset if others are allowed to laugh too much. We distrust uncontrollable laughter because total laughter dissipates the thoughts that control us. Most of us don't like to be out of control so we control our laughter.

We must recognize that laughter is the expression of our aliveness:

- Laughter is healing energy coming to the surface from deep within us to be shared with others.
- Genuine laughter is contagious and its healing is also contagious.

When we laugh thinking stops. Then energy follows through relaxation. When you can laugh with someone there is nothing the two of you cannot overcome. You become more powerful than any problem or event. Life and relationships are not to be taken seriously. In fact life is only truly understood, and best appreciated, when you are laughing. Laughter is a high state of consciousness present in humans and their immediate ancestors. Indeed, it may well be a path to our higher selves:

- Laughter may be the only true path to enlightened consciousness.
- When you are laughing you are love expressing itself.

Most of us, however, have been taught to value seriousness. Unfortunately, seriousness is often confused with sensitivity, concern, compassion, commitment and discipline. In our society we value "maturity" and, as proof, often demand a commitment to being serious about everything. At that point, to be happy is to be frivolous, hence wrong; to be serious is mature, hence right. The result is often misery, boredom and the feeling of being trapped.

Unfortunately, most have been taught that seriousness is a positive state to be held in high esteem and a commitment that is difficult but necessary in life. Seriousness is everywhere. And if everyone is serious, how can we be happy? We were born happy. As children all we thought about was our happiness. Adults mistake this behavior for selfishness because they are busy worrying about the world. This pattern carries into adult life and is often a major measure of adulthood. Be honest:

- How often have you resented the happiness of a child, a lover or a friend?
- How often have you been upset because someone in your life was having a good time?

Most adults don't believe the world, or life, to be especially joyful so that is how we indoctrinate our children. We ingrain in them a pattern of belief, which allegedly protects the child from misery. At the same time, in an almost calculating manner, we destroy the child's joy and aliveness.

From early childhood until adulthood our concept of happiness becomes:

- Hope, a code word synonymous with worry.
- Dependent upon money.
- Whatever happiness is, it cannot last.

Early in life we are told, "Don't be selfish." And slowly we accept the idea that the joy of happiness is wrong or at least lags behind every other consideration. We were told, "Always feel for and consider others." And are hence given the obscure message that if we suffer, "they" will be happy. Another old line is, "Eat everything on your plate because there are people starving in Africa." As if starvation would disappear if we ate more.

Religion, which should be joyous, was also presented to most of us in a serious tone and as something to be feared. We learned early, "You can go to hell for that." And we were told, "God will punish you."

Going to church was not an experience I enjoyed. The all-knowing, punishing and sermonizing was not something I wanted. I failed to find any humor except in retrospect. I suspected that Christianity came to be represented by the cross because, for many Christians, the cross represents pain, suffering and death. Few seem to recognize that the cross represents the transformation of Jesus becoming the Christ Consciousness.

I also suspected that Christ was a much more joyous man than we have been led to believe. We are told only of his seriousness, not his playfulness. Any person who likes food, wine and a lively conversation at dinner with friends must laugh. It is logical that Christ knew the joy of humor, yet there are no representations of him laughing. Your divine purpose in this life is to have a good time. Unfortunately, to be a Christian, Jew or Muslim, and to be happy at the same time, is nearly a contradiction in terms.

Most of us were taught that the world is a miserable place and in order to be part of it, to be in tune with it, we must be miserable at least once in a while. And that to be happy, joyous and laughing is to be insensitive, thoughtless or even cruel to those who are busy being miserable. This is why we often feel guilty or hold back our laughter in moments of happiness. Our minds are conditioned to work this way.

Sex really gets to be serious stuff. Most civilized Earthlings make love as if they are on duty. We often hide having a good time, afraid to lose control in the ecstasy, refusing to surrender to our pleasure and happiness. Or we are content emulating romantic fantasies reminiscent of a scratchy rerun of the "From Here to Eternity" beach scene.

It is no wonder people are unhappy. Imagine being so serious that you deprive yourself of the satisfaction of orgasm. A lot of people still do. And even if they have an orgasm, they are serious about getting it. Their minds are saying, "It doesn't look right. What will my partner think? What if the children hear?" They may even feel guilty, which is actually the fear that others might disapprove of their enjoying sex.

We have even managed to create guilt without sex, so either way you lose. "With or without sex, by all means be serious" is the destructive message.

On the other hand, those who enjoy sex:

- Cry.
- Shout.
- Laugh.
- Giggle.
- Scream.
- Dramatize.
- Talk.
- And play.

They are alive when enjoying the behavior that created their aliveness. They are never sure what emotions will surface. But most still think it is better to be in control or otherwise they may look foolish. And, of course, "What would God think of all this pleasure?" Hundreds of thousands of people report feeling dissatisfied after sex. They are caught between two dilemmas: If they let go they feel guilty; if they withhold they are deprived and they feel guilty about that. This then provides the possibility of being angry with their partners and blaming others for their dissatisfaction.

After all our conditioning a certain willingness to let go is required to stop being serious and calculating. When you are happy and suddenly the serious voice in your head starts interfering with your pleasure, ignore it. Allow it to die. Never give seriousness any more attention than simple observation of what it is. Attention creates form that becomes food for thought that strengthens your attention that increases your seriousness.

Instead of all this mental static simply listen to your laughter. Become immersed in laughter and you will move closer to your aliveness. When we are expressing aliveness, we do not experience seriousness, pain or guilt. Let seriousness play its hand and we are moving away from our aliveness toward death.

When we are laughing, boundaries and limits fall away. Our energy merges with existence and we disappear into life itself.

- Don't attempt to be happier or to laugh more.
- Stop rehearsing and just be.
- Become more conscious and the natural by-product will be laughter.
- Be totally absorbed in your life, in your aliveness, and laughter will suddenly be there.

Laughter is a surprise. A happy person never thinks about being happy. Happiness and laughter are not connected with our thoughts. They are beyond the brain. They are states of being.

- Stop chasing laughter. When you do this you are just being serious about catching something that cannot be caught.
- Move into action in the moment and your ego will be replaced with laughter.
- Retreat from your significance as frequently as possible and become aware that "you are significant" is a ridiculously overstated circumstance and realize that you are indeed unique.
- Stop attending to everything. The art of happiness and laughter requires some selective forgetfulness.

The greatest crime committed against relationships is the idea that they should be serious. Being serious about your relationships destroys your relationships.

- Instead, be sincere.
- Be thoughtful.
- Be considerate.
- Be compassionate.
- But give up being serious. Seriousness is a disease you don't need.
- Seriousness may well prove to be the mother of all disease.

An alive, healthy person cannot be serious. Only people who have cut their roots and become disconnected from existence can be serious. When you uproot a rose bush it dies. When you pull a fish from water it dies. When you stop laughing you die.

- Risk and move from fear to laughter.
- Listen to the children. Learn from them and they will benefit from what you learn.
- Realize the truth that laughter is the forgotten prayer. God, and all that exists, hears you each time you laugh.
- Eliminate your relationships that condemn laughter.
- Realize that when you and your lover laugh, there is nothing to discuss, there is no need for words.
- Stop modeling these serious, dead relationships. A relationship not reborn regularly with a good laugh is dying.

When you laugh totally, you heal and cleanse yourself. For a moment we are an innocent child again, full of wonder. Then a deep, sudden silence comes like the moments after a storm. This is a signal that the brain has paused. You are relaxed, rested and absent of thought. Let yourself appreciate existence more often. Notice your aliveness. And when you find yourself getting really serious about life, take another look and laugh knowing that life and laughter are inseparable.

Live in laughter.
Even among those who are serious.
Hug someone.
Even among those who are frightened.
Dance with yourself.
Even among the couples.
Laugh out loud.
Even among those who think a lot.
Sing in the shower and on the street.
Even among the deaf.
Laughter has to be shared.
That sharing of laughter is love.

∞

Quality 19

Relatedness

You are the only consistent factor in your life. Everyone and everything else comes and goes. When you notice that there is only a handful of other people who have been in your life from the beginning until now you realize these people are special, that you love them and that they love you. You love these people enough to allow them to transform within your relationship with them.

Others come and go. They change and move on. That is also perfect as it is. If everyone you met stayed in your life the probability of new people making new contributions would diminish. People are supposed to come and go, healing them selves and you through your mutual relatedness. They are supposed to share pieces of their life with you then move on and make space for other people to heal and contribute to you.

Relatedness: No beginning, no end, only change in relationship; connected, in communication with someone or something by choice.

Just imagine if everyone stayed in your life. Imagine the size of your address book, all of the birthdays, weddings and funerals. Why then do we surrender our reality and get upset each time someone leaves our lives? Because we think "the end" rather than "completion and acknowledgement." Our lives and our relationships are in continuous transformation. This is the key. Relationships change form continuously. Transformation is the ability to have an experience beyond form. The secret is to:

- Have that awareness.
- And expect transformation.

Then there is aliveness and respect for each other. We suddenly and simply experience people without insisting that there be a beginning, middle or an end to the relationship. We then have people in our life we do not insist on defining. Relationships become long-term and fascinating. There is a connection, an excitement, an adventure and we respect each other. When we become available we stop separating from other people. We quit worrying that they are not in the form we prefer. The contemporary mind thinks in terms of a beginning, middle and an end. It has to do this in order to function, get things done, go through school or work, to complete a task and to survive the physical universe.

It requires some practice to experience our life with no beginning, middle or end. But as we move in that direction our life will begin to take on all kinds of new meaning. Aliveness occurs, which you remember having as a child, except this time the aliveness is consciously created.

When this quality of no beginning or end exists in our relationships, we will allow them to transform. One benefit is that children can grow up to become friends with their parents and parental approval is no longer the basis for that relationship. The judgments disappear and you get to be with each other as you are.

We transcend the obvious, and we will see the thread, the connection that runs through everything in your life. We will change dramatically. We will come to realize what Einstein knew: "You cannot begin something that has already begun nor end something which is endless." Einstein transformed the way we think about our world. He helped confirm that life is experiential.

Most of us, however, ensconced as we are in our agenda of judgments, define something and then do it. Or we stop experiencing and meander toward death with constant conclusions. In fact, that is when the death process starts happening and when the aliveness starts disappearing. The secret to getting beyond that kind of rut is to do something and let the conclusions arrive through the experience. With this method, you begin to see a definite connection, an "implicit order."

- We relate beyond the biology of things.
- We choose not to relate to men as men and women as women.
- We do not relate to others as "wealthy" or "poor" as Europeans or Americans, or black or white.

We see those differences, of course, and we appreciate them, but what we value is not so explicit. We value the implicit. That connection is who we truly are. When we see that and experience relatedness in our relationships they will be affected. Some will be stronger and more joyful. Others may dissipate. We might even get a divorce.

If that happens, of course, pain will revolve around the experiences you shared such as children and feelings and pets. My experience of most children is that they can move through the pain of a separation. It is the parents who have difficulty. At first children may be shocked by divorce and perhaps even think they are the cause. But what they really fear is losing the implicit love of one or both of the parents.

Children see:

- The thread.
- The relatedness.
- The connection.
- The implicit.
- The love.

And when children are reassured that both parents love them and are going to continue to love them they can handle this transformation called divorce. Children change games, but keep friends. Adults tend to get rid of friends and loved ones in order to keep the game going. This is because most adults in contemporary society are more invested in form than in people.

We are all being human. And, while we must focus and see form in order to function, we must also realize that we really are transforming. We can experience this any way we choose. When we do not lose sight of that thread of relatedness:

- The thread becomes love and respect for other people regardless of their current transformation and form.
- Rather than fearing the end of relationships we willingly complete them, creating new and exciting experiences.
- New forms emerge with that same person we value and create new connections to other people they value.

Ultimately, we become aware of who we truly are, which is part of a network of people that comprise a group much in the same way as stars comprise a galaxy that is part of an expanding universe.

∞

Quality 20

The Presence of Love

When we "fall in love" it is an illusion. Yes, it makes us happy, validates us and we get to experience having achieved something. When we "fall out of love" that is also an illusion. It makes us sad, humiliates us and we loose something. Romantic love as a permanent state is illusion. Real and alive relationships may appear romantic and the people in them may express the joy we usually consider romance. The difference is that romantic love has no choice but to become exploitative. Those who "fall in love" usually love others that have little to give. Encouraging the act of "falling in love" is like calling disease healthy.

Love: The absence of all negative thought and emotion, to be empty. When we are aware of the presence of love within us:

- Love is sufficient unto itself and without attachment.
- We recognize that love attached to anything ceases to be love and becomes manipulation.
- We experience ourselves as love, so loving others just happens. We are beyond judgment.
- We are clear that our relationships are just extensions of our love.
- We are more alive.
- Our sexual experiences have the quality of love and intimacy just happens.
- We receive love from many sources and that allows us to give love to many, even though, out of ignorance, some may be un able to love you.

- We have only loving relationships, which opens us to our self and to others, rather than pseudo-loving ones that shut us down and narrow our experience of others and life.

Love is a present-time phenomenon. When projected into the future love dissolves into disillusion. The secret is to love and to beware of making the promise of love. There are two general definitions that can be given to love:

- "Falling in love" and that depends on others.
- Experiencing our self "as love" and an expression of who we are.

Romantic love fosters lovesickness, which is love pulsating with crisis and trauma. All we think about is the object of our affliction. There is weeping and crying, waiting, fantasizing, jealousy and perhaps even violence. All are substitutes for real relationships in which you have the opportunity to be love. For all that has been made of romance in countless books and films, the reliance on romantic love is actually the avoidance of love as these substitutes are constructed by those unwilling to consciously experience themselves as love.

Real love is like a ray of light from a lamp shining into darkness. The source of light needs space to glow and needs freedom to grow. Experiencing yourself "as love" is authentic and absent of need. In this experience, we are as loving alone as we are with someone else. It is like singing in the shower with no one to hear you.

Love is sufficient unto itself. Your love can never be possessed or owned by another. Love is not a commodity. Being love is constant and conscious. It is yours to share. Love is independent of our partner's needs yet it is involved with each of you as you share each reality. In time your experience of each other's weaknesses melts and your limits become your mutual challenge. Being love requires being there for your partner all the time. This is only possible when your self-love is so abundant that it overflows to our lover. A relationship that is alive is:

- To be love together.
- To experience the power of consciously choosing to share yourself with someone else.
- To be willing to receive their love for as long as you both choose to share. There is no achievement greater than this. It requires a growing awareness and the willingness to communicate.

Somehow we can always manage to admit that our past loves were illusions, but not the present one. We say, "This one is true. This is the real thing." When this one passes we may again admit it was an illusion unless we really go into it and become aware of our love together. But we don't usually do that. Normally we prefer to delude ourselves and believe at last we have found our one true "soul mate."

No one has ever found a "soul mate." Souls recognize the boundlessness and absolute nature of love. Souls do not need mates. But that may seem too simple or too controversial, as our culture has invested heavily in the illusion of soul mates. So, we "fall in love" as this is a familiar state. We have done this many times. For example, you may have loved:

- Your mother and father.
- Your cat or dog.
- Your friends.
- Your new car.
- Your jewelry.
- Your favorite ice cream, etc.

We have all "fallen in love" with people or pets or possessions.

Only the objects of the illusion have changed. When "falling in love" dissipates, and it does, we move toward the reality of consciously being alone. We soon, however, begin to unconsciously experience being alone as loneliness. When the discomfort of loneliness becomes too great we move toward the illusion of "falling in love" again. If "in love" is true, how can loneliness be false? If "together" is true, how can alone be false? Our eventual experience of "falling in love" in fact will be loneliness.

When you choose "falling in love" you have chosen one polarity of a total experience. To achieve a relationship that is alive you must recognize this seemingly never-ending wheel of change, pay close attention and be willing to move on. If you continue chasing romantic rainbows you will become exhausted. And you will never experience the satisfaction of real love.

Once you have had enough of the tedious, culturally driven illusions of "falling in love," you will begin to see that:

- "Falling in love" is the avoidance of self because you are choosing to dissolve into someone else.
- You are love itself and are surrounded by illusions. With this realization you can choose to be in a relationship that thrives on romantic and creative moments yet does not linger in the illusion and fog of romance.
- You are in a relationship that does not require distraction or demand consolation.

Consider this parable on the play of light and darkness: Darkness came to God and said, "Please. I am exhausted. Everywhere I go light follows. It's all I can do to stay ahead of her. Please God, tell the light to give me a break and leave me alone."

God said, "Okay, I'll see what I can do."

As darkness disappeared, light appeared. And God said, "Listen, darkness was just here telling me how exhausted he is from all your chasing and harassing. Do you think you could leave darkness alone and simply appreciate and enjoy him?"

Light appeared puzzled and said, "God, what are you saying? Where is this darkness? Show me, because I know nothing of darkness."

God smiled at light and said, "Okay, you may go."

When you are light, you see no darkness. When you are love, you see no loneliness. Loneliness occurs only when you love someone more than yourself. Love does not know:

- Loneliness.
- Jealousy.
- Possessiveness.
- "Falling in love."

Make the choice to be your own source of love. When you do this you will experience being the ocean rather than simply another ripple of a wave crashing on some lonely beach. Love is your natural state of consciousness.

- Love is like breathing.
- It is your heartbeat.
- It is the blood circulating through your body.
- Love is your very being, your core and your source.

Love is the absence of all negative emotion. Love is a fragile energy, a subtle presence that is often obscured by the heavier energies of emotion. This fragile energy can be destroyed because most of us don't recognize or acknowledge the presence of love. We may pretend and become afraid to admit to anyone that we don't know. And while we live in this illusion we live with others living in the same illusion of not knowing what love is.

Love is an art in a world with few artists. We are born with the capacity and the potential to love. We are not born, however, with the ability to express our love. Few of us can communicate our love with care and accuracy. While each of us is born with a body, few learn to dance and fewer still are capable of learning to dance with another person. The harmony required to dance with another is created by choice, not by accident. So it is with love.

You must learn to be love and to teach your body to be a lover. Stop waiting and start loving. The only way to learn how to love is to love. You just have to do it.

And, like anything else, you will improve with experience. Never miss an opportunity to love because you are waiting for the "right" person. Love and be available to love and you will learn the art of loving. By doing this you will attract others with whom you can share the process of conscious love.

In considering conscious love without attachment we should recognize the many types of love that we have the opportunity to experience. I have come to appreciate those with whom I have shared real love and the alternative types of relationships as well.

• The Fun-Fast: This generally happens when traveling or at a dinner party the last night in town. It's always a fantastic experience and to think about it reduces it to something less than it was. This is one of those rare experiences that if repeated becomes anti-climactic. It is not something you do. It does you.

- The Serious-Fast: This kind of relationship usually occurs in a strange or new location, maybe even with someone who doesn't speak your language. The moment is dominated by a building intensity. This kind of love usually transforms you, but it also has the potential for pain because if one of you is in a Serious-Fast mode while the other is in Fun-Fast then anger, loss and rejection may soon follow. This type takes months to get over and usually creates a pattern of rejecting anyone remotely similar for a long time.

- The Fun-Slow: This is like floating because you both seem to walk on air. You fit so well that you lose sight of your contributions to each other. All your friends and family approve. This one is so rare that it may happen only once or twice in a lifetime. You usually experience this when you are young, optimistic and romantic. This can become chronic because, if you are young and naive, you don't value the beauty of the experience and may never get over it. This is also the type you try to reclaim when you are older and wiser, but this is a challenge because you have become more sophisticated and complex.

- The Serious-Slow: This is the one that society and the people in power have a vested interest in you desiring and, even worse, doing. This is the one that's meaningful, significant, entangled, at times tedious and treacherous, but ultimately worthwhile, whatever that means. It's reasonable and boring and everyone wants that for you. This is the one fewer and fewer people are doing twice in their lives. But this voice keeps saying, "Do it again," and some people can't help themselves.

It's time to create a new experience, a fifth alternative, that is both fast and slow, both fun and thoughtful, never serious yet always conscious. It's time to be lovers and friends in relationship. That's when:

- You are in love and don't sacrifice one friend. They come along with you like a rich dowry.
- You are together by choice, not coincidence, circumstance or duty.
- Any doubts expressed transform into trust, caring and sharing.
- Fear of intimacy and commitment dissolves because you realize you're so in love there is nowhere else you want to be.
- You are having satisfying sex with a sexually experienced friend. When you're together, performance and worry dissolve into passion and laughter.
- You are compassionate and willing to serve each other except when it feels like duty and obligation.
- Anger and disagreement don't threaten your love and friendship.
- Mutual boredom or insecurity melts in an embrace.
- Your lover's mere existence creates within you a sense of well being and belonging.
- Your respect for each other overcomes any embarrassment you cause each other.
- You are companions, fellow travelers on the road of life.
- You don't take turns following each other. You mirror each other.
- You travel through life with each other, whether you are apart or together.
- Over time a friend evolves, even when your companion is a lover.

Only when you have experienced this type of love will you under-stand completely what it means. Until then, be aware. Should such a lover appear, allow that person to be your friend as well as your lover. Be lovers and friends. When you are lovers and friends you see some-thing of yourselves in each other. If that something is criticized, it becomes an opportunity to heal each other. You embody each other's values. Conscious lovers:

- Laugh, joke and play in bed.
- Love the way the other looks, smells, feels and touches.
- Know that sexual pleasure is a gift to enjoy and to celebrate.

When conscious lovers are friends a special quality emerges. This quality is trust, though not the kind that comes from promising to trust each other. Rather this is a trust, which occurs as a by-product of knowing each other.

- Real trust cannot be created any other way.
- In an alive relationship doubt eventually transforms into acceptance.
- Immediate promised trust is illusion and is actually naive "blind faith."

When lovers are friends:

- No faith is needed. Trust is the foundation for friendship and must also be the foundation for love.
- They choose one another.
- Choice is a preference rather than an expectation.
- The fragility of their love is supported by their trust.

In love there is always the element of risk. Once you have been hurt you may choose to "never love again" because you may feel you can never trust again. It may even appear easy when you have been hurt by love to give up and make independence a way of life. But before you decide on that route, recognize that independence goes nowhere. Independence is the new word for lonely. Taken to its furthest extreme, it is a death before dying primarily because there is no growth in independence. Such a retreat from life will destroy your own spirit because you will ultimately have stopped trusting yourself. If, however, you are interdependent and in touch with your own inner strength and self-trust you will always be surrounded by lovers and friends.

In conclusion, always remember go beyond conditional and unconditional love. Be a lover. What is most important is to love and to learn to trust. If there is disappointment, pain or betrayal, reach out to a lover and friend. You are at your best when you reach out and trust someone. You are guaranteed ecstasy when you risk without guarantees. Trust yourself and the process of life.

About Frank Natale

Frank Natale was founder and creative director of Frank Natale & Associates, an experiential education organization presenting seminars throughout the United States, Europe and Australia. Natale's teaching emphasized self-awareness, personal responsibility and choice as paths to conscious living and spiritual growth.

Books by Frank Natale include *The Wisdom of Midlife, Relationships for Life*, and *Trance Dance, The Dance of Life*.

"Most paths of self-correction purposely increase the effort and struggle to achieve these states or vibrations," Natale wrote in his foundational course Results: The Willingness to Create. "They insist that you must 'earn it' or 'handle it' or 'surrender to it' or 'get it' when the truth is you already have immediate access to all of it. You, in fact, are an aspect of it. The illusion we have created that we are separate from our source robs us of the direct experience of the intimacy and aliveness of our higher selves."

Life Skills seminars created by Frank Natale include Trance Dance, Dance of Life; Rites of Passage, The Circle of Life; The One Experience; Honorable Sexuality; Alive Relationships; Creative Communications; Self Esteem, The Power Within; Results: The Willingness to Create.

Natale was committed to the healing dance practices of indigenous cultures since the early days of The Esalen Institute where he became friends with Gabrielle Roth, the founder of 5Rhythms. In the 1990s Natale, with his band Professor Trance and other collaborators, produced a body of music to drive the Trance Dance experience including the albums Shaman's Breath, Medicine Trance, Rites of Passage, Dance Your Animal, Spirit Animal, Breath of Fire and Dancers of Eternity.

Om Bilateral Alignment and Ambient Om meditation albums were dedicated to Baba Muktananda, Natale's spiritual teacher.

A native New Yorker, in 1967 Natale co-founded Phoenix House in New York, which became the largest residential treatment facility for chemical dependency in the United States. After serving as clinical director for twelve years, Natale chose to leave Phoenix House and focus his work on successful, functioning personalities who want to experience new levels of spirituality, creativity and aliveness.

During the Sixties and Seventies Natale studied and worked with many leaders of the modern human consciousness movement including Charles Dederich, Abraham Maslow, Carl Rogers, Fritz Perls, Baba Muktananda, J. Krishnamurti and Buckminster Fuller.

Frank Natale lived a conscious life and died a conscious death. He passed in Hawaii on his birthday in 2002 surrounded by family and friends.

Natale books and music are available on Amazon.com, iTunes and other digital platforms. For more, visit FrankNatale.com.

www.ingramcontent.com/pod-product-compliance
Lightning Source LLC
LaVergne TN
LVHW021449080426
835509LV00018B/2222